THE
WEIGHT LOSS SURGERY
COOKBOOK COLLECTION

200+ | Of The Best Recipes From
The Essential Weight Loss Surgery
Cookbook & The Weight Loss Surgery
Slow Cooker Cookbook

LASSELLE PRESS CO

LASSELLE PRESS Cº

© Copyright 2017 by Lasselle Press

All rights Reserved. No part of this book may be reproduced in any form without permission in writing from the author. Reviewers may quote brief passages in reviews.

Limit of Liability / Disclaimer: No part of this publication may be reproduced or transmitted in any form or by any means, mechanical or electronic, including photocopying or recording, or by any information storage and retrieval system, or transmitted by email without permission in writing from the publisher. While all attempts have been made to verify the information provided in this publication, neither the author nor the publisher assumes any responsibility for errors, omissions or contrary interpretations of the subject matter herein. The information in the book is for educational purposes only. It is not medical advice and is not intended to replace the advice or attention of health-care professionals. This book is sold with the understanding that the publisher is not engaged in providing legal, medical or other professional advice or services. Consult your physician before beginning or making any changes in your diet. Specific medical advice should be obtained from a licensed health-care practitioner. The Publisher will not assume any liability, nor be held responsible for any injury, illness or personal loss due to the utilization of any information contained herein. Adherence to all applicable laws and regulations, including international, federal, state and local laws governing professional licensing, business practices, advertising and all other aspects of doing business in the US, Canada, UK or any other jurisdiction is the sole responsibility of the purchaser or reader. Lasselle Press publishes its books in a variety of print and electronic formats. Some content that appears in electronic books may not be available in print, and vice versa.

ISBN-13: 978-1911364528
ISBN-10: 1911364529

CONTENTS

INTRODUCTION | 10

C1: WEIGHT LOSS (BARIATRIC) SURGERY OVERVIEW | 11

C2: YOUR DIET & NUTRITION | 19

C3: POST-SURGERY DIET RECOMMENDATIONS & FOOD LISTS | 23

C4: EATING OUT & TRAVELING | 31

LIQUID RECIPES | 35

Vegetable Consommé 36
Chicken Consommé 37
Milky Chai Latte 38
Homemade Smooth Vegetable Soup 39
Homemade Clear Chicken Soup 40
Milky Hot Chocolate 41

SOFT & PURÉED RECIPES | 42

Puréed Banana Oats 43
Homemade Low Fat Yogurt 44
Mixed Bean Purée 45
Protein Turkey and Brown Rice Purée 46

BREAKFAST | 47

Savory Bread Pudding 48
Hearty Shakshouka 49
Protein-Packed Breakfast Bars 50
Melting Tuna and Cheese Toasties 51
Vegetarian Spinach Tortillas 52
Rustic Bean & Mushroom Hash 53
Fresh Apple & Quinoa Breakfast 54
Spiced Pumpkin Breakfast Bars 55
Banana & Chia Seed Breakfast 56

Avocado & Berry Breakfast Bowls 57
Spiced Sweet Potato Muffins 58
Banana and Honey Muffins 59
Cheesy Egg Slices 60
Golden French Toast 61
Breakfast Berry Wrap 62
Flourless Breakfast Muffins 63
Punchy Protein Pancakes 64
Hot and Fluffy Strawberry Pancakes 65
Rise and Shine Protein Smoothie 66
Soft Oats with Strawberry Jam 67

SEAFOOD | 68

Grilled Dorades with Arugula Salad 69
Asian-Style Steamed Monkfish 70
One-Pan Cod and Cauliflower in a Spiced Tomato Sauce 71
Airfried Mackerel with Gingered Brown Rice 72
Herring Salad 73
Sardine Salsa 74
Salmon Portabello Burgers 75
Tuna Sashimi with Lime-Chili Quinoa 76
Seared Salmon Fillets and Sautéed Leeks 77
Salmon and Sweet Corn Soup 78
Seared Teriyaki Salmon with a Black Bean and Green Mango Salad 79
Tuna and Veggie Fritters 80
Potato and Cod Stew 81
Baked Lemon and Parsley-Crusted Sea Bass 82
Thai-Style Cod en Papillote 83
Chinese-Style Halibut with Wild Rice and Bok Choy 84
Tilapia, Garlic, and Tomato Bake 85
BBQ Sole Fillets with Parsley, Mint, and Tomato Salsa 86
Grilled Cod with Sweet Potato Mash and Cumin Yogurt 87
Low Fat Fish Tacos with Kale Leaves 88

VEGETARIAN | 89

Provençal Ratatouille 90
Veggie Chili 91
Crunchy Super Salad 92
Refreshing Zucchini and Parsley Noodles 93
Airfried Carrot and Zucchini Fritters 94
Roasted Fennel with Apple Cider Glaze 95
Truffle Cauliflower Bake 96

Lime-Roasted Eggplants   97
Grilled Tomatoes with Black Garlic Spread   98
Tomato and Arugula Egg White Scramble   99
Sunshine Pie 100
Kale Fruit Salad   101
Savory Tofu   102
Baked Sweet Cabbage   103
High-Protein Scrambled Eggs   104
Peppered and Herbed Egg Muffins   105
Tomato and Herb Pizettes 106
Spinach and Mozzarella Bake   107
Luxurious Cauliflower Cheese   108
Fresh Chickpea Salad   109

POULTRY | 110

One-Tray Chicken and Kale Bake 111
Zucchini Pasta with Ground Turkey and Fresh Peaches   112
Slow Cooker Polenta and Turkey Curry   113
Salt and Peppered Grilled Chicken   114
Grilled Chicken and Caprése Sandwich   115
Airfried Chicken Satay with Cucumber Salsa   116
Hoisin Chicken Cabbage Wraps   117
Airfried Chicken Kebabs   118
Shredded Chicken and Berry Salad   119
Marinated Paprika Chicken   120
Baked Parmesan & Herb Coated Chicken Strips   121
Juicy Jerk Chicken   122
Chicken Simmered With Black Beans 123
One Dish Greek Baked Chicken   124
Red Wine Chicken   125
Sweet and Tangy Chicken with Pumpkin Purée   126
Low-Carb Chicken Tortillas 127
Stuffed Chicken   128
Cheesy Chicken and Cauliflower Bake   129
Chicken and Lotus Root Soup   130
Stuffed Cubanelle Peppers   131
Airfried Herbed Chicken Breasts with Balsamic Cherry Tomato Salad   132

SOUPS, STEWS & STOCKS | 133

Weight Loss Fish Stock   134
Collard Greens Soup Topped with Sage Mushrooms   135
Carrot and Potato Soup   136
Red Pepper and Tomato Soup   137
Slow Cooker Chicken Soup with Baby Spinach Leaves   138

Thai Chicken Soup   139
Cherry Tomato Soup   140
Curried Zucchini Soup   141
Rutabaga and Sweet Potato Soup   142
Slow Cooker Chicken Curry 143
Slow Cooker Chicken Chili   144
Roast Turkey Breasts with Brussels Sprouts   145
Slow Cooker Chicken and Lemon Rice Stew   146
Fennel and Ginger Chicken with Asparagus Tips   147
Carrot and Turkey Soup   148
Turkey Goulash with Baby Spinach Leaves   149
Cabbage Soup with Arugula Leaves   150
Cumin and Turmeric Fish Stew   151
Super Greens Soup   152
High Protein Chickpea and Garden Pea Stew   153

SAUCES & CONDIMENTS | 154

Creamy Basil Pesto   155
Cannellini Hummus   156
Baba Ganoush Dip   157
Homemade BBQ Sauce   158
Mixed Bean Salsa   159
Spicy Lentils   160
Parsley Hummus   161
Spicy Mango Chutney   162
Peach and Mango Salsa   163
White Cheese Sauce   164

SNACKS & SALADS | 165

Thai 'Rice Noodle' Salad   166
Cucumber and Sundried Tomatoes   167
Spiced Lentils on a Baby Spinach Bed   168
Edamame and Avocado Dip   169
White Wine Chicken and Spinach Salad   170
Ginger Quinoa with Balsamic-Roasted Brussels   171
Cucumber Bites Stuffed with Lemon-Dill Cottage Cheese   172
Nutella® Protein Bars   173
Zucchini Bread   174
Rice Cooker Quinoa   175
Parsley Sautéed Mushrooms   176

DRINKS | 177

Chocolate Drink   178
Homemade Soy Milk   179
Guava Milkshake   180
Blueberry and Vanilla Protein Shake 181
Strawberry and Vanilla Smoothie   182
Pineapple and Guava Juice

183
Vanilla Cafe Latte Shake 184
Black Forest Dream Smoothie 185
Strawberry, Cucumber and Kale Vanilla Milkshake 186
Chocolate and Banana Smoothie 187

DESSERTS | 188

Apple Cake 189
Pecan Cookies 190
Vegan Strawberry Crumbles 191
Pumpkin Cheesecake 192
Easy Crépes 193
Healthy Chocolate Mousse 194
Strawberry Frozen Yogurt 195
Lemon and Lime Sorbet 196
Low Fat Pana Cotta 197
Blueberry Yogurt Cups 198
Poached Pears with Rosemary Red Wine Reduction 199
Pumpkin Pancakes with Apple Compote 200

SLOW COOKER RECIPES

BREAKFAST | 202

All-Ready Oat Porridge 203
Delightful Vegetarian Enchiladas 204
Light & Fluffy Frittata 205
Delicious Quinoa & Plum Porridge 206
Layered Vegetable Frittata 207
Chicken Spinach & Red Pepper Omelet 208
Cream of Wheat Goodness 209
Hempseed Breakfast Bowl 210

POULTRY & SEAFOOD | 211

Thyme Turkey with Curly Kale 212
Mild Chicken Curry 213
Chicken & Summer Squash 214
Turmeric Sweet Orange Chicken 215
Leek, Fennel & Dill Chicken Stew 216
Spanish-Style Chicken 217
Spiced Caribbean Chicken 218
Turkey & Lemon Risotto 219
Moroccan-Style Apricot Tagine 220
Slow Cooker Rice Wine Chicken 221
Barbecue Pulled Chicken 222
Roast Chicken & Stuffing 223
Slow-Cooked Chicken in Red Wine Sauce 224
Chicken & Rice Broth 225
Slow Cooker Lean Turkey Tortillas 226
Slow Cooked Stuffed Peppers 227
Slow-Cooked Meatballs with Tomato Sauce 228
Italian Chicken Stew 229
Slow-Cooked Chicken Thighs with

Sweet Potato & Mango 230
Tomato & Green Olive Cod Stew 231

VEGETARIAN | 232

Super Squash Stew 233
Mediterranean-Stewed Vegetables 234
Slow-Cooked Chunky Root Veggies 235
Soft Red Cabbage & Cranberry Sauce 236
White Cabbage & Lentils with Relish 237
Herby Root Veg & Quinoa 238
Roasted Pepper, Spinach & Lime Quinoa 239
Greek Rice & Tzatziki 240

SOUPS, SIDES & STOCKS | 241

Spicy Carrot & Lime Soup 242
Coconut & Lemongrass Turkey Soup 243
Turkey & White Cabbage Soup 244
Low Fat Vegetable Broth 245
Low Fat Chicken Broth 246
Mixed Herb Marinade 247
Citrus Rice & Beans 248
Mashed Beets 249

Sweet Onion Relish 250
Honey & Mustard Glazed Root Veg 251

DESSERTS | 252

Strawberry & Peach Crumble 253
Sugar-free Applesauce 254
Easy Rice Pudding 255
Poached Spiced Apples & Pears 256

DRINKS & SHAKES | 257

Immune Booster Shake 258
Leafy Protein Smoothie 259
Chia Berry Boost 260
Carrot & Ginger Smoothie 261
Homemade Tomato Juice 262
Marvellous Mango Shake 263
Peach Iced-Tea 264
Super Green Shake 265
Apple & Banana Smoothie 266
Banana & Nut Butter Shake 267

CONVERSION TABLES | 268

REFERENCES | 270

INDEX | 273

INTRODUCTION

INTRODUCTION

Welcome to The Weight Loss Cookbook Collection!

Whether you're considering weight loss surgery, are preparing for it now, or you've had surgery already, it can be a particularly confusing and challenging time in your life. Not only will you have to go through surgery, you will have to change your diet and lifestyle before and after your operation. What to eat, how much, when and how, are probably just a few of the questions you're asking, not to mention having to decide which of the weight loss surgeries is the best choice for you.

That's why we've put together over 200 recipes from both The Essential Weight Loss Surgery Cookbook and The Weight Loss Surgery Slow Cooker Cookbook in this huge collection to keep you inspired in the kitchen and losing the weight you want to after your surgery. All of these recipes have been designed for post weight loss surgery, please always consult your doctor for specific guidance as each person's recovery diet will be unique to them. That being said, these recipes are provided with their nutritional content, use easy-to-find and healthy ingredients, and are delicious. You won't feel like you're missing out with these recipes, and the slow cooker recipes are great for busy lifestyles or bulk cooking.

We have also included an overview of the three main types of bariatric surgery - the gastric sleeve, the gastric bypass, and the lap band. We explore the different stages of diet and recommendations for pre and post surgery. Helpful lists of foods to continue enjoying as well as those you should avoid are given, to help you with your grocery shopping and meal plans. Furthermore, we hope that our lifestyle hints and tips for dining out, traveling and cooking will be helpful in getting started and sticking to your weight loss goals post surgery.

We wish you all the best on your weight loss journey and know that with the right diet and lifestyle, along with the determination to succeed - your goals are possible!

Happy cooking,

The Lasselle Press Team

C1: WEIGHT LOSS (BARIATRIC) SURGERY OVERVIEW

So Why Get Weight Loss Surgery?

Perhaps you've tried everything to lose weight, possibly most of your adult life, and nothing seems to have worked. Maybe you've developed an emotional relationship with food; one that you turn to when you're feeling down or stressed out. Or it could be that you've struggled with your weight all your life and you just need the support, education and guidance that bariatric surgery offers.

All this being said, weight loss surgery is not the easy way out as many critics might believe. So many people view it in this way, but what they don't realise is that it takes a lifetime of care and healthy choices to maintain weight loss, and that surgery alone is not the answer! Additionally, there is the matter of going through major surgery in itself. This requires a patient to completely adjust their lifestyle and diet both before and after.

That being said, weight loss surgery can provide you with the confidence and mindset you need to be able to lose more weight and keep it off long term. This is because, depending on the type of surgery you have, you will not be able to either consume or absorb as many calories as you did prior to surgery. Furthermore, the education, psychological support and assistance that you will be given, when implemented with dedication, can help change your relationship with food and excess weight forever. This will not only help with healthy weight loss but also work to prevent many other health risks that are associated with obesity.

The Different Types of Weight Loss Surgery

There are three main types of weight loss surgery, each with their own pros and cons. The following information will summarise each procedure, as well as points to take into account when considering which type of surgery is best for you.

1. The Gastric Sleeve

Surgery Time = 1 hour
Hospital Stay = 2 to 3 days
Recovery Time = 2 to 4 weeks

If you have been considering weight loss surgery for a while, you have most likely heard of the gastric sleeve, but what is it exactly? The Gastric Sleeve is a restrictive operation that will make your stomach smaller. This is what helps people lose weight as you will feel full much more quickly. Rather than suffer through starving yourself on a diet, it will help you to make the lifelong necessary change of eating smaller portions.

The gastric sleeve is performed through abdominal incision or by making several smaller incisions and using a camera to guide the surgery. Once the incision has been made, about half or more of your stomach is removed from your body, leaving a tube that is about the size of a banana. This surgery is irreversible.

Why The Gastric Sleeve?

This surgery is best suited for you if:
- You are severely overweight and have tried to lose weight but can't, even with exercise, diet, and medication,
- You have a body mass index of 40 or higher or -
- There is a life-threatening issue that requires you to lose weight.

However, remember that surgery is a tool to help you lose weight - not an instant fix. You will need to eat the right type of foods as well as exercise after your surgery to lose weight and then maintain that weight loss.

What Is The Success Rate?

According to studies, 80% of patients have lost up to 50% of their excess weight after their gastric sleeve surgery and kept it off for at least 5 years. This success rate is based on the patients who followed the eating plan, were physically active, and were realistic about how much weight they needed to lose. Weight loss will take dedication even after the surgery.

What Are The Risks?

After surgery, vitamins and minerals may not be properly absorbed due to the restricted size of the stomach. Other risks during surgery include infection from the incision, a blood clot in the lungs or gallstones, or a nutritional deficiency such as anemia. That being said there are risks with any type of surgery and these should be weighed up, with a professional, against the potential quality of life post-surgery.

What Are The Benefits?

Gastric Sleeve Surgery:
1. Can help to reduce hunger,
2. Does not involve operating on your intestines,
3. Has a shorter operating time than other weight loss surgeries,
4. Does not require adjustments after surgery,
5. Helps with weight loss over an 18 month period.

How Much Will It Cost?

On average, the cost of the gastric sleeve is around $19,000. Depending on where you are located, it could range from $4,000 to $60,000. It should be noted that this cost will not include your pre-op, post-op, or any complications that may occur. Please note that there are financing options available that will help pay for your surgery if needed.

2. Lap Band Surgery

Surgery Time = Less than 1 hour
Hospital Time = 1 to 2 days
Recovery Time = 10 days

Lap band surgery involves tying an adjustable gastric band around your stomach to make it smaller. It limits the amount of food your stomach can hold. This will help you eat less, become fuller after smaller portions, and ultimately lose weight faster.

This surgery is performed through small abdominal incisions, through which the surgeon will insert a camera to monitor the surgery and tie the band around the upper section of your stomach. The ring around your stomach will be attached to a thin tube that leads to an access port under your skin. This access port will be where your doctor can add and/or take away saline with a needle; the saline is needed to tighten the band to make your stomach smaller. Likewise, the saline will be removed if the ring is too tight.

Why Lap Band Surgery?

This surgery is best suited for you if:
- You are severely overweight and have tried to lose weight but can't, even with exercise, diet, and medication,
- You have a body mass index of 35 or higher or -
- You suffer from a disability due to your weight.

Again, remember that surgery is a tool to help you lose weight - not an instant fix. You will need to eat the right type of foods and exercise after your surgery to lose weight ad then maintain that weight.

What Is The Success Rate?

The success rate is not as high as the gastric band surgery at around 47% of those losing more than 50% of their excess weight and keeping it off for 5 years after the surgery, compared to 80% of gastric sleeve patients.

What Are The Risks?

1. Access port problems: there is a risk of getting an infection in the access port. The port could also disconnect, leak, or become blocked.
2. Esophageal dilation: this issue will occur if your band is too tight. It could also happen if you are eating too much. When this happens, your esophagus could expand and make it hard for you to swallow.
3. Band slippage: for some patients, the band can slip out of place. When this happens, symptoms such as belly ache and heartburn can occur. It is treated by removing fluid in the band. Unfortunately, this could lead to having to have a second operation.
4. Obstruction: food can sometimes block the opening of the stomach, causing, nausea, pain, or vomiting.
5. GERD: Another risk of lap band surgery is developing gastroesophageal reflux disease.

What Are The Benefits?

1. Minimal trauma- the least invasive option,
2. Fewer risks and side effects,
3. Adjustable surgery,
4. Reversible- can be removed at any time,
5. Effective for long-term weight loss.

How Much Will It Cost?

On average, the cost of a lap band is around $15,000. Depending on your location, it could range between $4,000 and $33,000. This price will vary based on your insurance. There are also other ways to afford the surgery including discounts and other financing options.

3. Gastric Bypass Surgery

Surgery Time = 1.5 hours
Hospital Time = 2 to 3 days
Recovery Time = 2 weeks

Gastric bypass is a procedure that will alter the way your body digests food. The surgery works in two ways: first, it will help with restriction, limiting the amount of food you can consume by reducing stomach size. Second, the surgery will limit the absorption of food by bypassing a section of your small intestine. This combination aids weight loss.

Why Gastric Bypass Surgery?

This surgery is best suited for you if:
- You are at least 100 pounds overweight,
- You have tried to lose weight but can't, even with exercise, diet, and medication,
- You have a body mass index of 40 or higher or -
- You suffer from an obesity related disease.

Once again, remember that surgery is a tool to help you lose weight - not an instant fix. You will need to eat the right type of foods and exercise after your surgery to lose weight and then maintain that weight.

What Is The Success Rate?

The success rate is one of the highest at around 85% losing more than 50% of their excess weight and keeping it off for 5 years after the surgery.

What Are The Risks?

1. Potential allergic reaction to medication,
2. Gastritis,
3. Heartburn or stomach ulcers,
4. Injury to stomach or other organs during surgery,
5. Scarring inside stomach,
6. Vomiting from overeating,
7. Dumping syndrome- occurs when a lot of food moves in to the stomach too quickly,
8. Internal bleeding from surgical wounds,
9. Bowel obstruction.

What Are The Benefits?

1. Reduces obesity-related illnesses (including diseases such as diabetes, sleep apnoea, and even high blood pressure).
2. An improved quality of life e.g. a decreased risk of depression and anxiety, improved self-esteem etc.
3. Long term weight loss - for those who opt for the gastric bypass, they may find that the weight loss post surgery will not only be rapid, but it will also continue over months and years later.
4. A quick recovery time.

How Much Will It Cost?

On average, the gastric bypass surgery can cost anywhere from $15,000 to $35,000 depending on your location. Again, this price will vary based on your insurance. There are also other ways to afford the surgery including financing options.

C2: YOUR DIET & NUTRITION

As you already know, surgery is not a one stop fix to weight loss; there will be changes you will need to make both before and after your surgery. These changes will be life-long in order to lose your target weight and maintain that weight loss. This chapter will outline key pre and post operation tips.

Pre-Surgery Guidance:

- Eat your meals evenly throughout the day,
- Drink throughout the day- a minimum of 2 liters,
- Do not drink alcohol,
- Take a multivitamin daily (as recommended by your surgeon).

Diet Plan Before Surgery - Recommended Daily Portions Broken Down:

1. Carbohydrates =3 portions
2. Fruit = 2 portions
3. Vegetables = 3-5 portions
4. Protein = 2 portions
5. Milk = 2 portions
6. Keep calories between 800-1000 kcal per day depending on height, weight and surgeon's guidelines.

Serving Size Equivalents

The following lists will help you understand how much is included in a given serving so that you don't go over the recommended serving sizes and portions each day.

Remember that the pre-op diet recommends:

Portions Per Day=
Carbohydrates=3
Protein =2
Fruit =2
Veg = 3-5
Milk = 2

Carbohydrates Example Portion Sizes:

1 Portion =

- 1 medium slice of bread or toast
- 2 small potatoes (boiled or mashed) or 3 petite potatoes with skin
- 5 tablespoons of all-bran
- 2 tablespoons of boiled rice
- 1/2 Weetabix
- 3 tablespoons of boiled pasta
- 2 rich tea biscuits
- 3 tablespoons of bran flakes, fruit & fiber or cornflakes
- 1 digestive biscuit
- 3 tablespoons of dry porridge oats
- 1/2 bagel
- 4 tablespoons of Rice Krispies
- 2 small oat cakes

- 1 crumpet
- 1/2 pita or 1 small pita
- 2 crisp breads

Proteins Example Portion Sizes:

1 Portion =

- 4 ounces of lean cooked meat
- 2 ounces of low fat soft cheese/low fat cheese/low fat cottage cheese
- 4 ounces of cooked white fish or canned tuna (in spring water or brine)
- 2 medium eggs (maximum of 6 per week) - poached, boiled or scrambled
- 1 small skinless chicken breast
- 4 tablespoons of cooked peas, lentils, beans (including baked beans, kidney beans etc.)
- 4 ounces of tofu or Quorn products

Fruits Example Portion Sizes:

1 Portion =

- 1 medium piece fresh fruit e.g. 1 apple
- 2x small fruits e.g. plums, satsumas
- 5 ounces of strawberries
- 3 tablespoons of stewed or canned fruit (no added sugar)
- 5 fluid ounces of fruit juice (no added sugar)

Vegetables Example Portion Sizes:

1 Portion =

- 3 heaped tablespoons of cooked vegetables e.g. tomatoes (canned or fresh), eggplant, beets, cabbage, spinach, broccoli florets, zucchini, cucumber, fennel, leek, lettuce, watercress, mushrooms, radish, peppers, scallions, rutabaga etc.
- 3 heaped tablespoons of salad
- 1 large tomato or 7 cherry tomatoes
- 6.5 fluid ounces of tomato or vegetable juice (unsweetened)

Dairy Example Portion Sizes:

1 portion =

- 6 1/2 fluid ounces of skim milk
- 1 small pot of non fat or low fat yogurt

C3: POST-SURGERY DIET RECOMMENDATIONS & FOOD LISTS

Foods To Enjoy Long Term (After Recovery Stages)

Post-Surgery Guidance

After surgery, you could experience multiple symptoms. These include body aches, dry skin, mood change, hair loss, and feeling tired or cold. These should go away as your body gets used to the weight loss and it will definitely be worth it in the long run!

Depending on the type of surgery you've had as well as a variety of other factors including, age, weight, weight loss goals and recovery stages, your diet will usually begin with clear liquids, progress onto puréed foods, then soft foods and then small portions of 'real' foods. This always needs to be planned with your post-surgery team and/or doctor. The lap band usually has the quickest recovery time, meaning you will likely move on to solids within the shortest period of time after surgery. However this should always be approached slowly and with a professional's guidance.

Portion sizes will be much smaller than what you're used to immediately post surgery:
Liquids -generally recommended portion size = 2-3 fluid ounces.
Purées - generally recommended portion size = 5-6 tablespoons.

Please note that all puréed and solid foods should be introduced gradually. Likewise, the number of portions you can eat will depend on your stage of recovery, the type of surgery you have had, and a variety of other factors. Please always consult with your doctor or post surgery care team to ensure you're following a suitable plan.

General Guidelines - Portion Sizes After Recovery
1 serving =

Food	Amount
Fish	3 Ounces
Chicken/ Meat	3 Ounces
Cooked/Raw Vegetables	½ Cup
Sweet/Baked Potato	1
Cereal	1 Cup
Avocado/ Peanut Butter	1 Ounce/ 2 Tablespoons
Bread	1 Slice
Salad Dressing/ Olive Oil	1 Tablespoon

Meal Size General Guidance-

Each meal should be no larger than the size of your fist.

Grains/ Starches -

Stick with a single serving per day. The grains and starches food group is an excellent source of fiber, energy, B vitamins, minerals, and complex carbohydrates. Stick to whole wheat flour or whole grains including:

-Whole Wheat English Muffins
-Low fat Saltine Crackers
-Oatmeal
-Cream of Wheat
-Brown Rice
-Soy Crisps

-Melba Toast
-Corn
-Potatoes
-Yams
-Winter Squash

Vegetables -

Vegetables are essential to your diet. This food group will provide vitamin A, vitamin C, energy, and fiber. Aim for at least four servings of vegetables per day including:

-Broccoli florets (not stalks)
-Carrots
-Green Beans
-Asparagus (tips not stalks)
-Spinach
-Peppers
-Mushrooms
-Cauliflower
-Lettuce
-Olives
-Avocado

Fruits -

Include 2 to 3 servings of fruit per day. This will help provide vitamin C, energy, and fiber to your diet. Just be sure to introduce fruits slowly into your diet including:

-Berries
-Bananas
-Kiwi
-Orange
-Peach
-Plums
-Melon
-100% Fruit Juice

Dairy-

Aim for two servings of dairy a day. This will help provide your body with vitamin D and calcium including:

-Skim, Fat-Free, 1% Milk
-Low fat Yogurt
-Low fat Cheese
-Low fat Cottage Cheese
-Eggs

Spices/condiments -

Salt, pepper, fresh or dried herbs, spices, mustard, curry powder, lemon/lime juice, vinegar, yeast extract, fish sauce, soy sauce, Worcester sauce, OXO or other stock cubes, vanilla and other essences.

Healthy Fats (in moderation) including:

-Avocado
-Salmon
-Nuts
-Sardines
-Nut butters
-Coconut oil

Protein Shakes -

While you are recovering from weight loss surgery, protein shakes are a great meal replacement pre and post-operation.

Choose :
-Whey or soy based protein powders
-14g sugar or less per serving.
-5g of fat or less per serving.
-At least 10g of protein per serving.

Add to shakes, yogurt, breakfast oats or cereal **(only if these foods are included in your stage of recovery).**

Potential Problem Foods Post-Surgery

Please note that each patient is unique and foods that may cause problems for one person, may not necessarily cause any issues for another. That being said the following is a list of the foods that seem to cause more problems in general than others. Introducing new foods one by one and keeping a food journal, where you track foods and any symptoms experienced, can really help you identify the foods that do and do not agree with you. Always consult your doctor for specific guidance.

Foods To Avoid Long Term

Vegetables and fruits that contain stringy fibers can be problematic including:

- Fresh Pineapple
- Broccoli Stalks– the stalks may be problematic so cut these off before cooking
- Dried Fruits – can swell inside your body and should be avoided
- Oranges – flesh may be problematic
- Asparagus Stalks
- Rhubarb
- Large Cuts Of Meat – if consuming meat, chop very small and chew thoroughly
- Coconut (difficult to digest)
- Crisps (difficult to digest)
- Soft White Bread (difficult to digest)
- Nuts (such as peanuts, almonds, walnuts) and popcorn may also cause obstructions and are best avoided
- Greasy And Spicy Foods

- Whole Milk
- High Sugar Foods,
- Cakes, Biscuits And Desserts
- High Calorie Drinks (Full Milk, Milkshakes, Alcohol, Fruit Squashes)
- Cereals With Added Sugar
- Fats And Fatty Foods – Butter, Oils, Packaged Snack Foods
- Creamy Soups
- Beef
- Pork
- Shellfish
- Grapes
- Whole Grains
- Corn

Top Tips For Diet & Lifestyle After Your Surgery

1. Only eat three small meals a day,
2. Eat solid foods,
3. Eat slowly and stop eating as soon as you feel full (this may be further up in your chest before the sensation reaches your stomach),
4. Cut your food into very small pieces, then chew each piece as many times as possible before swallowing,
5. Don't overeat (or eat too fast) so as to avoid unpleasant symptoms, such as pain and vomiting,
6. Don't drink during meals. This can flush food out of your stomach pouch and make you feel less full. Avoid drinking fluids 15 minutes before a meal and 45 minutes afterwards,
7. Avoid drinking high-calorie drinks, such as cola, alcohol, sweetened fruit juices and milkshakes. These types of drinks quickly pass out of your stomach and into your small intestine, increasing your calorie intake,
8. Ideally just drink water,
9. You will get most of your calcium requirements from three portions of dairy food each day,
10. Consume 48 to 64 ounces of fluids per day - sip throughout the day and avoid eating and drinking at the same time,
11. Avoid using straws and chewing gum as this might trap air in your pouch causing discomfort and bloating,
12. Remember, your diet is just part of your lifestyle - exercise regime must be implemented and stuck to if you want to keep the weight off. Try to exercise for at least 20 minutes per day. Not only will this help you lose and maintain weight loss, it also comes with a whole host of physical and mental health benefits!

C4: EATING OUT & TRAVELING

Advice For Dining Out:

You don't have to miss out on your favorite restaurants or cuisines for the rest of your life!

Follow these tips to stay healthy and ensure you don't gain back those hard earned weight losses!

1. Look out for small, half portions or side dishes and ask your server for your foods to be cooked without extra salts, butters or sauces.
2. Avoid fried foods and opt for grilled or poached instead.
3. If you know you are going out to eat, plan ahead: look at the restaurant's menu beforehand and decide what you will order to avoid anxiety or stress on the night.
4. Use the food lists in the previous chapter to help you choose and don't feel bad about asking them to cater for your needs.
5. Ensure you have eaten your other meals before you go out for dinner, or time brunch or lunch well so that you can pace out the rest of your meals for the day.
6. Remember to avoid ordering drinks during your meal. Instead you could take it easy after you've eaten and then order a healthy drink.

Advice For Traveling:

Whatever your travel plans, you will have to eat. The following tips should help make this easier for you:

- If you plan ahead, you should be able to make a meal plan to suit your needs.
- If you have a dietitian, tell them where you are going and what you expect to eat at your destination so they can help you with this,
- Remember to pack any multi vitamins you take and continue to take them daily - put a reminder on your phone as it's so easy to forget when traveling, especially across time zones.
- Avoid eating unhealthy snacks by packing healthy options such as fruits, rice crackers and low fat cheeses when you go out for the day,
- You could also take meal replacement drinks to replace a meal when you're out and about and potentially won't be able to find anything suitable.
- If going on a road trip or camping, avoid processed meats. If at all possible, use fresh-cooked meats, reduced sodium deli meats, unsalted chicken or tuna.
- Remember to track your calories - apps such as My Fitness Pal allow you to do this on the go. Or do it the old fashioned way and read the labels! Just remember to write it down!
- If you are going on a cruise, all those buffet foods can be tempting to tuck into 24 hours a day. To help with this predicament try to select fresh fruits, salads, and vegetables.
- Remember to include a good source of protein with every meal.
- If you are going to be traveling abroad and don't speak the language, take a phrasebook that has a section for ordering food.

Cooking Tips:

1. Grill, poach, roast or sauté lean meats instead of frying,
2. Steam or boil vegetables instead of frying,
3. Use healthy oils such as extra virgin olive oil instead of butters and vegetable oils.

One Last Thing:

Always remember to only use new recipes and ingredients after speaking to your doctor or dietitian; your needs will be unique to you depending on the type of surgery you underwent as well as how your body has recovered. We hope that with your doctor's advice, along with our guidance and recipes, that you can continue to enjoy cooking, eating and sharing meal times with your love ones as well as losing the weight you set out to lose!

Please note:
It is crucial you see your dietitian to determine the amount of calories you should be consuming each day and adjust the serving sizes according to your individual requirements if necessary.

All nutrition levels have been calculated using The US Department of Agriculture's Super Tracker website www.supertracker.usda.gov and may differ depending on specific brands. It is always advised to track your nutrition using a tracking site such as this one or by studying the individual labels on foods.

We wish you all the best on your weight loss journey.
Happy cooking!

the essential WEIGHT LOSS SURGERY COOKBOOK

155 | 155 Delicious Recipes To Be Enjoyed After Weight Loss Surgery

LASSELLE PRESS CO

LIQUID RECIPES

Vegetable Consommé

SERVES: 3 / PREP TIME: 10 MINUTES / COOK TIME: 50 MINUTES

A silky clear consommé perfect for your liquid diet as well as for use in thicker recipes later on. Suitable for vegetarians.

2 egg whites
14 oz. vegetable stock

- Whisk the egg whites until just starting to foam.
- Add the egg whites to the vegetable stock until smooth.
- Add the stock to a deep pan over low heat.
- Bring to a boil until the egg whites form a crust on the surface.
- Line a sieve with muslin or a clean tea towel (not washed in soap or detergent) and scoop the egg white crust on top.
- Very gradually ladle the stock through the egg whites and sieve until all of the liquid runs through (don't push this through).
- Return the liquid to the pan and heat until hot (don't boil again).

Per serving: Calories: 20 Protein: 4g Carbs: 1g Fiber: 0g Sugar: 1g Fat: 0g

Chicken Consommé

SERVES: 4 / PREP TIME: 10 MINUTES / COOK TIME: 50 MINUTES

A silky clear consommé perfect for your liquid diet as well as for use in thicker recipes later on.

2 egg whites
16 oz. homemade chicken stock

- Whisk the egg whites until just starting to foam.
- Add the egg whites to the chicken stock until smooth.
- Add the chicken stock to a deep pan over low heat.
- Bring to a boil until the egg whites form a crust on the surface.
- Line a sieve with muslin or a clean tea towel (not washed in soap or detergent) and scoop the egg white crust on top.
- Very gradually ladle the stock through the egg whites and sieve until all of the liquid runs through (don't push this through).
- Return the liquid to the pan and heat until hot (don't boil again).

Per serving: Calories: 51 Protein: 5g Carbs: 4g Fiber: 0g Sugar: 2g Fat: 1g

Milky Chai Latte

SERVES: 2 / PREP TIME: NA / COOK TIME: 10 MINUTES

A lightly spiced milky hot drink.

1/2 tsp. honey
1 tsp. black tea leaves, powdered
1/2 tsp. cinnamon
1/2 tsp. nutmeg
2 cloves
8 fl oz. almond/skim/soy milk

- Combine the honey, tea, and spices and mix well.
- Add the milk to a small pot over low heat.
- Bring to a light simmer and add the powder, mixing well continuously until the lumps have dissolved.
- Drop in the cloves, turn the heat to lowest, cover and allow to simmer for 10 minutes.
- Pour through a sieve to get rid of the cloves and serve in your favorite mugs.

Per serving: Calories: 62 Protein: 1g Carbs: 12g Fiber: 1g Sugar: 11g Fat: 1g

Homemade Smooth Vegetable Soup

SERVES: 4 / PREP TIME: 5 MINUTES / COOK TIME: 25 MINUTES

A wholesome dish made with high protein vegetables.

1/4 cup canned chickpeas
1/2 carrot
1/2 cup onion
3 cups vegetable stock/water
1 bay leaf
1/2 cup frozen peas
2 cups spinach leaves

- Add all ingredients to a pot (apart from peas and spinach) over medium heat.
- Bring to a rolling simmer, cover and continue to simmer for 20 minutes over low heat.
- Add the spinach and peas and simmer for a further 5 minutes.
- Remove from the heat and allow to cool slightly.
- Remove the bay leaf and discard.
- Process in a blender or using a hand blender until completely smooth.

Hint: You can add a swirl of skim or soy milk here to make a creamier soup.

Hint: Make in bulk and simply heat through when needed. Store in an airtight container in the fridge for up to 5 days and in the freezer for 2-3 weeks. Just ensure you allow to defrost thoroughly before heating again.

Per serving: Calories: 77 Protein: 6g Carbs: 13g Fiber: 5g Sugar: 0g Fat: 1g

Homemade Clear Chicken Soup

SERVES: 6 / PREP TIME: 5 MINUTES / COOK TIME: 40 MINUTES

A light and clear soup, great for post surgery meals or as a base for soup, stew, and broth recipes.

10 oz. skinless, boneless chicken breast
1/2 carrot, peeled and finely diced
1/4 cup zucchini, peeled and finely diced
1/4 cup onion, peeled and finely diced
3 cups chicken stock

- Add all ingredients to a pot over medium heat.
- Bring to a rolling simmer, cover and continue to simmer for 30-40 minutes over low heat.
- Ensure chicken is thoroughly cooked through before removing from the heat and allowing to cool slightly.
- Process in a blender or using a hand blender until completely smooth.

Hint: You can add a swirl of skim or soy milk here to make a creamier soup.

Hint: Make in bulk and simply heat through when needed. Store in an airtight container in the fridge for up to 5 days and in the freezer for 2-3 weeks. Just ensure you allow to defrost thoroughly before heating again.

Per serving: Calories: 125 Protein: 17g Carbs: 6g Fiber: 0g Sugar: 3g Fat: 3g

Milky Hot Chocolate

SERVES: 2 / PREP TIME: NA / COOK TIME: 10 MINUTES

A comforting hot chocolate drink that you can enjoy post surgery.

---

8 oz. almond/soy milk
1 tbsp. cocoa powder (unsweetened)
1 cinnamon stick

- Add the milk to a small pan over low heat.
- Bring to a light simmer and add the powder, mixing well continuously until the lumps have dissolved.
- Add the cinnamon stick, turn the heat to lowest, cover and allow to simmer for 10 minutes.
- Carefully remove the cinnamon stick.
- Remove from the heat and pour into your favorite mugs to serve.

Hint: Sweeten with a little Stevia or honey if permitted at your stage of recovery.

Per serving: Calories: 53 Protein: 1g Carbs: 10 Fiber: 1g Sugar: 8g Fat: 2g

SOFT & PURÉED RECIPES

Puréed Banana Oats

SERVES: 2 / PREP TIME: 5 MINUTES / COOK TIME: NA

A puréed breakfast, great post surgery.

1/2 banana
1/4 cup ground oats
8 oz. boiling water

- Peel and cut banana into slices.
- Steam bananas for 10 minutes.
- Mix boiling water and oatmeal in a separate bowl.
- Blend oatmeal and banana until you have a smooth consistency. You may add more water or oatmeal depending on your preferred consistency.
- Serve warm.

Per serving: Calories: 59 Protein: 1g Carbs: 14g Fiber: 2g Sugar: 4g Fat: 0g

Homemade Low Fat Yogurt

SERVES: 5 / PREP TIME: 9 HOURS / COOK TIME: NA

A homemade recipe for yogurt. You will need to buy a food thermometer for this which measures between 110-180°f

1 tbsp. yogurt starter (alternatively look for unflavored natural yogurt in the store) —must contain active cultures
1/2 liter skim milk

- Put a large pan of water (with a lid) on a high heat and bring to boiling point for 5 minutes.
- Add the thermometer and a spoon at this point to sterilize them.
- Now replace the water with the milk and warm through over medium heat until temperature reaches 185°f (this will ensure any 'bad' bacteria is killed).
- Keep the lid off while you're doing this to keep an eye on the milk.
- Don't let the milk boil!
- Remove the pan from the heat and allow to cool until it decreases to 110-115°f.
- Once at optimum temperature, stir the yogurt into the milk until completely mixed in and place the lid on top of the pan.
- Move the pan to a warm place (wrapped in a thick towel or in the airing cupboard works well). Leave at a constant temperature for a minimum of 9 hours and check up on it. It will become thicker the longer it is left.
- Allow to cool completely before transferring to airtight containers and store in the fridge for up to 3-4 days.

Approximate Per Cup: Calories: 137 Protein: 14g Carbs: 19g Fiber: 0g Sugar: 19g Fat: 0g

Mixed Bean Purée

SERVES: 2 / PREP TIME: 5 MINUTES / COOK TIME: 5 MINUTES

A high protein puréed meal.

---

1 oz. canned white beans
1/4 cup canned chickpeas
1 tbsp. water/soy milk

- Heat a skillet over low heat.
- Add the beans with the water and bring to a simmer.
- Lower the heat and simmer for 5 minutes (don't allow beans to boil).
- Remove from the heat, allow to cool slightly, and blend in a food processor or with a hand blender until smooth.

Per serving: Calories: 91 Protein: 6g Carbs: 15g Fiber: 4g Sugar: 2g Fat: 1g

Protein Turkey and Brown Rice Purée

SERVES: 4 / PREP TIME: 5 MINUTES / COOK TIME: 15 MINUTES

A puréed dish with a bit more substance!

1/2 cup carrots, washed, peeled and sliced
1 cup brown rice
1/2 cup cooked turkey cubes/slices

- Cook rice according to package directions.
- Place carrot in steaming basket with an inch or two of water in the bottom of a pan.
- Steam or boil for 10-15 minutes until tender, remove from heat and drain. If you are steaming keep an eye on water level as you may need to top up throughout to prevent drying out.
- Blend ingredients in a food processor, adding water as necessary for desired consistency.
- Serve warm.

Per serving: Calories: 98 Protein: 5g Carbs: 13g Fiber: 1g Sugar: 1g Fat: 3g

BREAKFAST

Savory Bread Pudding

SERVES: 4 / PREP TIME: 10 MINUTES / COOK TIME: 50 MINUTES

This dish combines a classic pudding with a savory twist.

---

4 slices diced wholemeal bread
1 red pepper, diced
½ red onion, diced
½ cup mushrooms, diced
2 cloves garlic, minced
3 eggs
1/2 cup skim milk

1 tsp. cumin
1/2 tsp. cayenne pepper
Black pepper, to taste
4oz. low fat mozzarella cheese

- Preheat the oven to 375°F.
- Grab a medium-sized bowl.
- Combine the bread, peppers, onion, mushroom and garlic.
- Whisk the eggs and milk in a separate bowl until well combined.
- Pour the egg mixture into the bread mixture.
- Add the seasoning and stir well.
- Pour the mixture into a lightly greased 4×4 baking pan.
- Sprinkle on the shredded cheese.
- Bake at 375°F for 40-50 minutes or until the eggs are set.

Per serving: Calories: 188 Protein: 18g Carbs: 19g Fiber: 3g Sugar: 6g Fat: 4g

Hearty Shakshouka

SERVES: 3 / PREP TIME: 5 MINUTES / COOK TIME: 25 MINUTES

This tomato-rich dish is full of fantastic Middle-Eastern and African flavors.

---

2 cloves garlic
1/2 green onion
Olive oil cooking spray
14.5oz. canned whole peeled tomatoes
A pinch of smoked paprika
1/2 tsp. ground cumin
½ tsp. dried oregano
¼ tsp. cayenne pepper

2 tbsp. soy protein powder
A pinch of salt and pepper to taste
6oz. can of mixed beans
3 large eggs
A handful of fresh parsley, chopped

- Mince the garlic and finely chop the onion.
- Cook in a large deep skillet with olive oil cooking spray over medium heat until soft and transparent (about 5 minutes).
- Add the canned tomatoes and their juices.
- Crush the tomatoes as you add them to the skillet
- Add the smoked paprika, cumin, oregano, cayenne, protein powder, salt, and pepper.
- Stir to combine.
- Allow the sauce to reach a simmer, stirring occasionally, for 5-7 minutes.
- The sauce should be thickened at this point.
- Drain the beans and add them to the skillet.
- Stir to combine.
- Return to a simmer.
- Simmer for 2-3 minutes more.
- Crack eggs into the skillet.
- Place a lid on top.
- Simmer for 5 minutes, or until the whites are set (the yolks should be soft).
- Top the skillet with the chopped parsley to serve.

Per serving: Calories: 337 Protein: 27g Carbs: 47g Fiber: 12g Sugar: 11g Fat: 5g

Protein-Packed Breakfast Bars

SERVES: 6 BARS / PREP TIME: 10 MINUTES / COOK TIME: 30 MINUTES

Full of delicious protein-rich ingredients to give you a boost of energy throughout the day.

1 cup porridge oats
1 tbsp. smooth nut butter
1 tbsp. coconut oil, melted
1 tbsp. agave/maple syrup
2 tbsp. whey/soy vanilla protein powder
1 tsp. ground cinnamon

- Heat the oven to 160°F.
- Grease and line the base of an 18 x 25cm tin with a little cooking spray.
- Mix the oats and nut butter in the tin.
- Place in the oven for 5-10 minutes to toast.
- Meanwhile, warm the coconut oil in a pan over low heat.
- Add the oat mix, syrup, protein powder, and cinnamon to the pan.
- Mix everything together until all the oats are well-coated.
- Tip into the tin, press down lightly, then bake for 30 minutes.
- Cool in the tin and cut into 6 bars.

Per serving: Calories: 121 Protein: 6g Carbs: 16g Fiber: 2g Sugar: 6g Fat: 4g

Melting Tuna and Cheese Toasties

SERVES: 4 / PREP TIME: 10 MINUTES / COOK TIME: 15 MINUTES

A perfect treat with tuna and golden, bubbling melted cheese.

6oz. canned line caught tuna in water
1 tsp. lemon juice
1/2 tbsp. olive oil
A pinch of sea salt and black pepper
1/4 cooked yellow corn
4 slices of whole meal bread
½ cup low fat cheddar

- Preheat your broiler/grill on its highest setting.
- Drain the tuna and flake into a bowl.
- Mix in the lemon juice and olive oil.
- Season with salt and freshly ground black pepper.
- Add in the corn.
- Toast the bread under the grill until it's nicely browned on both sides, then spread the tuna mixture on top, right up to the edges of the toast.
- Grate over the cheese and grill until the cheese is bubbling.
- Slice in half, grab a plate, and enjoy.

Per serving: Calories: 170 Protein: 15g Carbs: 14g Fiber: 2g Sugar: 2g Fat: 4g

Vegetarian Spinach Tortillas

SERVES: 5 / PREP TIME: 5 MINUTES / COOK TIME: 15 MINUTES

Tasty, cheesy, and full of flavor.

---

3 large eggs 2 tsp. skim milk
1/2 tsp. salt
1/2 tsp. garlic powder
1/2 tsp. dried cilantro
Olive oil cooking spray
1 cup fresh spinach, roughly chopped

1 cup canned kidney beans, rinsed and drained
5 small whole wheat tortillas
6oz. low fat cheese (mozzarella or cheddar)

- Whisk together the eggs, milk and seasonings in a large bowl and set aside.
- Spray a large skillet with cooking oil over medium heat.
- Add the spinach and allow to wilt for 1 minute.
- Add the beans, then pour in the eggs.
- Cook through, stirring occasionally until just set.
- Taste and season with salt and pepper as desired.
- Remove from the heat.
- Sprinkle a tortilla with 1/5 of the shredded cheese, leaving a small border all the way around the edge.
- Spoon 1/5 of the egg mixture on top, then fold in half.
- Repeat with the rest of the tortillas.
- To cook, carefully wipe out the skillet, spray once more with cooking spray, then heat over medium heat.
- Cook the assembled quesadillas on both sides until golden and the cheese is melted, about 5-6 minutes total.
- Cut into triangles and serve warm.

Per serving: Calories: 1247 Protein: 18g Carbs: 32g Fiber: 4g Sugar: 3g Fat: 5g

Rustic Bean & Mushroom Hash

SERVES: 4 / PREP TIME: 5 MINUTES / COOK TIME: 10 MINUTES

A warming dish with sweet shallots and smooth, fresh avocado. Heavenly.

16oz. canned kidney beans
Olive oil cooking spray
1 cup mushrooms, sliced
4 tbsp. shallots, minced
1 avocado, peeled and sliced
A pinch of pepper to taste

- Drain the liquid from the kidney beans.
- Cook the beans in a skillet over medium heat for 10 minutes (don't allow to boil).
- Meanwhile, spray a separate skillet with oil and add the mushrooms.
- Add the shallots.
- Cook for 5 minutes or until golden brown.
- Remove from the heat and to the pot with the beans.
- Remove the beans from the heat and set aside.
- Divide the bean mixture onto plates and top with the sliced avocado.
- Add pepper to taste.
- Enjoy!

Per serving: Calories: 156 Protein: 8g Carbs: 21g Fiber: 8g Sugar: 2g Fat: 5g

Fresh Apple & Quinoa Breakfast

SERVES: 4 / PREP TIME: 4 MINUTES / COOK TIME: 15 MINUTES

This wonderful South American grain is a great source of fiber, protein, and energy.

---

1 ½ apples, peeled and diced
2 tsp. ground nutmeg
2 tbsp. fresh lemon juice
2 cups water
1 cup uncooked quinoa
4 tbsp. skim milk

- Add the apples to a pot with the nutmeg and lemon juice.
- Bring the mixture to a boil over medium heat.
- Cook, stirring frequently, until apples are tender and have slightly caramelized.
- Remove from the pot with a slotted spoon and set aside.
- Add water and quinoa to the pot (without wiping it down).
- Cook the quinoa according to the packet directions.
- To serve:
- Add drained quinoa to 4 bowls.
- Top with the apples and swirl in 1 tbsp. milk.

Per serving: Calories: 192 Protein: 6g Carbs: 35g Fiber: 5g Sugar: 8g Fat: 3g

Spiced Pumpkin Breakfast Bars

SERVES: 4 BARS / PREP TIME: 10 MINUTES / COOK TIME: 30 MINUTES

Simple, delicious, and healthy – perfect for busy mornings or as a snack.

1/4 cup canned pumpkin purée
1/4 cup plain low fat yogurt
1 egg
2 tbsp. smooth peanut butter
1 tbsp. honey
1/2 tsp. nutmeg
1/2 tsp. vanilla extract

1/2 tsp. baking soda
1/4 cup dry rolled oats

- Preheat the oven to 375°F.
- Grab a large bowl and mix the pumpkin, yogurt, egg, peanut butter and honey together.
- Add the remaining ingredients and stir to combine.
- Pour the mixture into a greased 9x9 pan.
- Bake in the oven for 25-30 minutes.

Per serving: Calories: 113 Protein: 5g Carbs: 12g Fiber: 2g Sugar: 7g Fat: 5g

Banana & Chia Seed Breakfast

SERVES: 5/ PREP TIME: 5 MINUTES / COOK TIME: NA

An energy-packed bowl, also full of flavor.

---

2 medium ripe bananas
2 cups almond milk
1 tbsp. smooth peanut butter
2 tbsp. chia seeds
2 tbsp. soy protein powder

- Add all ingredients to a food processor or blender.
- Blend until well combined.
- Refrigerate for at least an hour.
- Serve.

Hint: You can leave it in the fridge for longer for a thicker consistency.

Per serving: Calories: 162 Protein: 7g Carbs: 24g Fiber:4g Sugar: 15g Fat: 5g

Avocado & Berry Breakfast Bowls

SERVES: 5 / PREP TIME: 5 MINUTES / COOK TIME: NA

Smooth, refreshing, and brilliantly nutritious.

1/2 avocado, peeled and diced
1 cup frozen raspberries
1 cup low fat Greek yogurt

- Combine all ingredients in a high-powered blender.
- Blend until smooth.
- Serve in cold serving cups or sundae glasses and enjoy.

Per serving: Calories: 132 Protein: 12g Carbs: 13g Fiber: 5g Sugar: 6g Fat: 5g

Spiced Sweet Potato Muffins

SERVES: 6/ PREP TIME: 10 MINUTES / COOK TIME: 25 MINUTES

This classic recipe has been switched up to create a tasty savory treat.

1/2 cup cooked, mashed sweet potato
1 egg
1/3 cup brown sugar
1/3 cup almond milk/skim milk
2 tbsp. coconut oil
1/2 tsp. nutmeg
3/4 cup whole wheat flour

1/2 tsp. baking soda
1/2 cup finely chopped red pepper
1 tbsp. paprika for sprinkling

- Preheat the oven to 375°F.
- Find yourself a large bowl.
- Combine the potato, eggs, sugar, milk, oil, and nutmeg.
- Mix until combined.
- Add flour and baking soda and stir until just combined.
- Mix in the red pepper.
- Scoop into 6 lined muffin tins and bake for 20-25 minutes.
- Hint: They're done when a toothpick inserted into the center comes out clean.
- Let them cool completely and sprinkle with paprika to serve.

Per serving: Calories: 120 Protein: 3g Carbs: 22g Fiber: 3g Sugar: 8g Fat: 5g

Banana and Honey Muffins

SERVES: 6/ PREP TIME: 10 MINUTES / COOK TIME: 22 MINUTES

Soft, warm muffins served fresh from the oven. Great with your morning coffee.

---

2 tbsp. coconut oil, solid
2 tbsp. honey
2 tbsp. almond milk (or other milk of choice)
1 egg
1/2 cup very ripe mashed bananas
1/2 tsp. vanilla extract

3/4 cup whole wheat flour
3/4 cup rolled oats
1/2 tsp. nutmeg
1/2 tsp. baking soda

- Preheat your oven to 375°F.
- Mix the coconut oil and the honey in a microwavable bowl.
- Microwave for 10 seconds at a time, stirring often, until the coconut oil is melted.
- Add the almond milk, egg, banana, and vanilla, and mix well.
- Add the rest of the ingredients and stir until just about combined.
- Pour into 6 lined muffin tins (to the top).
- Bake for 22 minutes.
- Hint: They're done when a toothpick inserted into the center comes out clean.
- Remove and cool on a wired rack before serving.

Per serving: Calories: 182 Protein: 4g Carbs: 29g Fiber: 3g Sugar: 9g Fat: 6g

Cheesy Egg Slices

SERVES: 4/ PREP TIME: 5 MINUTES / COOK TIME: 5 MINUTES

A power breakfast with a Mediterranean flavor.

---

3 large egg whites
A pinch of salt and pepper
1 tsp. oregano, dried or fresh
1 red pepper, finely sliced
4oz. low fat cheddar cheese

- Heat a skillet over medium heat.
- Grease with cooking spray.
- In a bowl, whisk the egg whites with the seasonings and red pepper.
- Pour the eggs into the skillet.
- Tilt the pan to spread the egg into a circle on the bottom of the pan.
- Cook for 1-2 minutes.
- Carefully flip with a large spatula and cook for another 30 seconds.
- Remove from pan and leave to cool slightly.
- Slice and serve with your choice of side - spinach leaves, grilled tomatoes, scallions.

Per serving: Calories: 103 Protein: 12g Carbs: 4g Fiber: 1g Sugar: 2g Fat: 4g

Golden French Toast

SERVES: 4 / PREP TIME: 5 MINUTES / COOK TIME: 10 MINUTES

A beautiful breakfast – serve with your favorite toppings.

---

4 egg whites
½ cup fat free soft/cream cheese
A pinch of salt
½ tsp. nutmeg
1 tsp. vanilla extract
4 slices of whole wheat bread
Olive oil cooking spray

- Beat the egg whites with a fork.
- Add the cheese, salt, and nutmeg and mix well.
- Add vanilla to the egg whites and mix until smooth.
- Dip the bread into the egg mixture, covering both sides.
- Fry in a nonstick skillet with cooking spray for 3-4 minutes on each side.
- Serve hot.

Per serving: Calories: 24 Protein: 12g Carbs: 15g Fiber: 2g Sugar: 3g Fat: 2g

Breakfast Berry Wrap

SERVES: 4/ PREP TIME: 5 MINUTES / COOK TIME: NA

A tasty swirl of creamy cheese and berries in a whole wheat wrap.

---

3 tbsp. fat free soft/cream cheese
3 tbsp. reduced sugar strawberry jelly
1 cup fresh, halved raspberries
4 small whole wheat tortillas

- Spread cheese and jelly on each tortilla
- Sprinkle sliced raspberries on top.
- Roll up the tortillas and enjoy!

Per serving: Calories: 162 Protein: 6g Carbs: 27g Fiber: 6g Sugar: 9g Fat: 4g

Flourless Breakfast Muffins

SERVES: 8 (1 MUFFIN EACH) / PREP TIME: 10 MINUTES / COOK TIME: 25 MINUTES

These muffins are light, fluffy and flavorsome; try baking these the night before to start your day the right way!

6oz. cooked chicken breast, diced (shredded broccoli works just as well for vegetarians)	1/4 tsp. dried oregano
2 large eggs	1/4 cup shredded low fat cheddar cheese
2 tbsp. skim milk	
1/4 tsp. salt	
1/4 tsp. pepper	

- Spray an 8-hole muffin tin with nonstick cooking spray.
- Preheat your oven to 350°F.
- Place 1/8 of the chicken pieces in each muffin cup.
- In a bowl, mix together the rest of the ingredients (apart from the cheese).
- Fill each muffin cup with 1/3 cup the egg mixture.
- Sprinkle the cheese on top of the muffins.
- Bake for 20-25 minutes or until the eggs are set.

Per serving: Calories: 56 Protein: 9g Carbs: 1g Fiber: 0g Sugar: 0g Fat: 2g

Punchy Protein Pancakes

SERVES: 5 / PREP TIME: 5 MINUTES / COOK TIME: 6 MINUTES

Just as indulgent as classic pancakes with an extra kick of energy.

---

1 cup whole wheat flour
1/2 tsp. baking soda
1/2 cup low fat soft/cream cheese
1 tbsp. coconut oil
3 large egg whites, lightly beaten
3 tbsp. soy protein powder

- Combine the flour and baking soda in a small bowl.
- Combine the remaining ingredients in another bowl.
- Pour the flour mixture into the cheese mixture.
- Stir until just combined – don't over mix.
- Heat a large skillet over medium heat.
- Give it a spray with cooking oil.
- Ladle batter into the skillet and swirl the skillet to form a mini pancake.
- Cook until little bubbles appear on the surface (about 4 minutes).
- Flip with a spatula and brown the other side for 1-2 minutes.
- Makes 5 mini pancakes.
- Serve with toppings of your choice or alone.

Per serving: Calories: 194 Protein: 16g Carbs: 25g Fiber: 3g Sugar: 7g Fat: 4g

Hot and Fluffy Strawberry Pancakes

SERVES: 4 / PREP TIME: 5 MINUTES / COOK TIME: 6 MINUTES

A classic breakfast with a light and fluffy texture.

1/4 cup low fat soft/cream cheese
1/4 cup instant oatmeal
1 tbsp. smooth peanut butter
2 large egg whites
1/2 cup fresh sliced strawberries
Coconut oil cooking spray

- Add the first four ingredients to a blender.
- Blend until a smooth pancake batter.
- Pour into a bowl and fold in the strawberry slices.
- Spray a skillet with cooking oil and heat over medium heat.
- Ladle in a pancake portion right in the center.
- Cook for 2-3 minutes on each side.
- Makes 4 pancakes.

Hint: Keep a plate in a warm oven to keep pancakes warm between batches.

Per serving: Calories: 74 Protein: 6g Carbs: 7g Fiber: 1g Sugar: 2g Fat: 3g

Rise and Shine Protein Smoothie

SERVES: 4 / PREP TIME: 5 MINUTES / COOK TIME: NA

This smoothie is super healthy and delicious - perfect for the first meal of the day.

1/2 eating apple
1/2 banana
2 tbsp. soy protein powder (whichever flavor you prefer)
1 cup spinach leaves
2 cups almond milk

- Peel and core the apples and cut into small chunks.
- Peel and slice the bananas.
- Tip into a blender, food processor, or smoothie maker.
- Add the protein powder, spinach, and almond milk.
- Pulse until smooth and well blended.
- Pour into small glasses to serve.

Per serving: Calories: 115 Protein: 6g Carbs: 19g Fiber: 1g Sugar: 16g Fat: 2g

Soft Oats with Strawberry Jam

SERVES: 3 / PREP TIME: 5 MINUTES / COOK TIME: 6 MINUTES

Creamy oats with sweet, tangy jam.

1.5 cups rolled oats
1/4 cup unsweetened almond or skim milk
1/2 tsp. vanilla extract

Strawberry Jam:
2 cups strawberries
4 tbsp. honey to taste
A pinch of ground nutmeg
1 tsp. lemon juice

- Place the oats in a bowl.
- In a separate bowl, mix the milk with the vanilla until fully combined.
- Stir the oats into the milk mixture.
- Cover and leave to soak overnight (or for at least 2 hours) in the fridge.
- Roughly mash the strawberries with a fork.
- To make the jam, mix the mashed strawberries with the honey.
- Pour this into a pan and gently simmer over low heat for 10 minutes.
- Add the nutmeg and squeeze in the lemon juice.
- Stir well and cook for 10 minutes until thickened.
- Cool, then chill in the fridge until you need it.
- To serve, layer the oats with 1 tbsp. jam into a bowl or jar, and top with a few extra strawberries if desired.

Hint: Store the rest of the jam in an airtight container in the fridge and use to top your favorite cereal, puréed fruits or a slice of wholegrain bread.

Per serving (1/3 oats + 1 tbsp. jam): Calories: 183 Protein: 5g Carbs: 34g Fiber: 4g Sugar: 5g Fat: 3g

SEAFOOD

Grilled Dorades with Arugula Salad

SERVES: 2 / PREP TIME: 10 MINUTES / COOK TIME: 20 MINUTES

The juicy fish is served with a peppery arugula side salad.

---

2 x 4 oz. dorade fillets
Juice of 1/2 lemon
9 cherry tomatoes
2 oz. canned anchovies
1 tsp. dried oregano
2 cups arugula leaves
1/2 tbsp. capers

- Preheat the oven to 400°F.
- Place the dorade fillets on aluminum foil sheets, and bake for 20 minutes, or until the fish is cooked through.
- To make the arugula salad:
- Combine the lemon juice, cherry tomatoes, anchovies, dried oregano, arugula leaves, and capers in a bowl, and chill until ready to serve.
- When the fish is cooked, top with the salad and its juices.

Per serving: Calories: 159 Protein: 27g Carbs: 5g Fiber: 1g Sugar: 3g Fat: 3g

Asian-Style Steamed Monkfish

SERVES: 2 / PREP TIME: 5 MINUTES / COOK TIME: 25 MINUTES

A light and savory monkfish, delightful for lunches and dinners.

---

2 x 4 oz. boneless monkfish medallions
1 stalk lemongrass, bashed and finely chopped
4 kaffir lime leaves
2 tbsp. chopped cilantro
2 tsp. shaoxing rice wine
1 tbsp. reduced sodium soy sauce
1 small ginger root, sliced
1 clove garlic, sliced
1 cup chopped scallions

- Arrange the monkfish medallions in a bowl that will fit the steamer snugly.
- Combine the lemongrass, lime leaves, chopped cilantro, rice wine, soy sauce, ginger slices, garlic slices, and chopped scallions in a bowl.
- Pour over the monkfish to cover.
- Steam for 20 to 25 minutes until the fish is cooked through.

Hint: If shaoxing rice wine is not easily available, substitute with a sweet sherry.

Per serving: Calories: 148 Protein: 23g Carbs: 6g Fiber: 1g Sugar: 1g Fat: 2g

One-Pan Cod and Cauliflower in a Spiced Tomato Sauce

SERVES: 2 / PREP TIME: 5 MINUTES / COOK TIME: 30 MINUTES

So easy to cook, and tastes sublime!

---

1 cup canned chopped tomatoes
1/4 tsp. ground cumin
1 tsp. ground ginger
1/2 tsp. ground turmeric
Freshly ground black pepper, to taste
6 oz. cod fillets
2 cups cauliflower florets

1 tbsp. chopped chives

- To make the tomato sauce:
- Combine the chopped tomatoes, ground cumin, ground ginger, and ground turmeric in a nonstick pan.
- Season with black pepper.
- Bring to a simmer over medium heat until the sauce has thickened slightly, about 10 to 15 minutes.
- Arrange the cod fillets and cauliflower florets in the tomato sauce, cover the pan with a tight-fitting lid, and continue to simmer over low heat until the fish is cooked through, and the cauliflower has softened.
- Spoon the sauce over the fish and vegetables.
- (During cooking, the fish should release its juices into the sauce, but if the sauce becomes too dry, add a little stock or water to pan.)
- Serve with a sprinkling of fresh chives.

Hint: Use a mix of broccoli and cauliflower florets for the veggies for a mix of color and texture. Add a dash of balsamic vinegar for a sweeter tomato sauce if desired.

Per serving: Calories: 123 Protein: 18g Carbs: 11g Fiber: 6g Sugar: 6g Fat: 2g

Airfried Mackerel with Gingered Brown Rice

SERVES: 2 / PREP TIME: 10 MINUTES / COOK TIME: 25 MINUTES

The salty taste of mackerel is balanced with a lime and soy rub, and paired with a ginger-infused earthy long-grain brown rice.

1 tbsp. reduced sodium soy sauce
1/2 tsp. lime juice
5 oz. mackerel fillets
1/2 cup uncooked long-grain, brown rice
1 tsp. grated ginger
2 tbsp. chopped chives

- Preheat the Airfryer to 350°F.
- Combine the soy sauce and lime juice to make a marinade.
- Rub the mackerel fillets with the mixture.
- Allow the fish to rest for 5 minutes.
- Arrange the mackerels in the Airfryer Basket, and set the timer for 20 minutes, or until the fish is cooked through, flipping over halfway through the cooking time to allow for even cooking.
- Meanwhile, cook the ginger flavored brown rice:
- Wash the rice until the water runs clear. Submerge the grains in 3/4 cup water, and stir in the grated ginger.
- Bring to a boil, cover, and reduce the heat for 20 minutes or until most of the water has been soaked up.
- Remove the mackerel from the airfryer and flake with a knife and fork.
- Serve the flaked airfried mackerel with a portion of brown rice, and top with the chopped chives.

Hint: If you don't have an airfryer, preheat the broiler/grill to medium heat and place the mackerel on a lined oven sheet for 10 minutes each side or until thoroughly cooked through.

Hint: If desired, add a dash of salt to water before bringing the rice to a boil.

Per serving: Calories: 117 Protein: 8g Carbs: 9g Fiber: 1g Sugar: 0g Fat: 5g

Herring Salad

SERVES: 2 / PREP TIME: 5 MINUTES / COOK TIME: 15 MINUTES

A festive favorite now made possible as part of a weight-loss diet, by replacing the potato staple with fresh cucumbers.

3 1/2 oz. water	3 oz. herring fillets
Juice from 1 lime	1 cup cubed cucumbers
3 1/2 oz. dry white wine	
1 tsp. white peppercorns	
2 bay leaves	
1 tbsp. white wine vinegar	
1 tsp. salt	

- To cook the herring:
- Combine the water, lime juice, white wine, peppercorns, bay leaves, white wine vinegar, and salt in a pot, and bring to a rolling boil.
- Reduce the heat to a simmer, and poach the herrings for 12 minutes, or until cooked through.
- Drain from the water and set aside to cool slightly. Flake with a knife and fork.
- Serve with the freshly diced cucumbers.

Hint: Add shallots, carrots, and celery to the cucumbers to make a heartier salad dish.

Per serving: Calories: 143 Protein 8g Carbs: 5g Fiber: 1g Sugar: 2g Fat: 6g

Sardine Salsa

SERVES: 2 / PREP TIME: 5 MINUTES / COOK TIME: NA

An easy to prepare and tasty salsa, perfect as a quick snack.

---

3 oz. canned sardines in tomato sauce
1 cucumber, peeled and diced
3 tbsp. chopped shallots

- Use a fork to flake the sardines into a salad bowl.
- Combine with the cucumber and shallots.
- Cover, and chill for at least 5 minutes for the flavors to blend before serving.

Hint: For a warm version of this dish, pour the sardines with their juices and the shallots in a nonstick pan. Bring to a simmer until the sardines are warmed through. Serve with the cucumbers.

Per serving: Calories: 109 Protein: 9g Carbs: 5g Fiber: 1g Sugar: 3g Fat: 6g

Salmon Portabello Burgers

SERVES: 2 / PREP TIME: 10 MINUTES / COOK TIME: 25 MINUTES

Salmon patties served on a whole portabello mushroom.

---

4 oz. salmon fillets, skinless and boneless
1 small ginger root, sliced
1/4 cup cilantro leaves
1 cup chopped celery
1 medium red capsicum, chopped
4 large portabello mushrooms

Freshly ground black pepper
Olive oil cooking spray
Juice of 1 lemon
1 cup arugula leaves

- To make the salmon patties:
- Pulse the salmon fillets, ginger, cilantro leaves, celery, and capsicums in a food processor.
- Scrape out the mixture from the food processor using a spatula, and then using wet hands, form 2 patties.
- Heat a nonstick pan over high heat.
- Grill the portabello mushrooms on the pan, until they shrink slightly.
- Remove from the pan, and season with black pepper.
- Heat another nonstick pan to medium heat, and lightly spray it with the cooking spray.
- Pan-fry the salmon patties until they are cooked through on both sides.
- To assemble:
- On each portabello mushroom, layer a salmon patty, drizzle over some lemon juice, sprinkle with arugula leaves, and top with another portabello mushroom.

Hint: If possible, charcoal-grill the portabello mushrooms for an added smoky flavor.

Per serving: Calories: 128 Protein: 16g Carbs: 10g Fiber: 2g Sugar: 5g Fat: 3g

Tuna Sashimi with Lime-Chili Quinoa

SERVES: 2 / PREP TIME: 5 MINUTES / COOK TIME: 20 MINUTES

A weight-loss version of the well-loved Chirashi recipe, with a lime and chili quinoa to spice things up.

1/2 cup quinoa
1 cup low sodium chicken stock
2 tsp. grated lime zest
1 tsp. cayenne pepper
Juice of 2 limes
6 oz. raw sashimi-quality tuna, thinly sliced (ensure this is from your fishmonger or fish counter and is appropriate for serving raw)

- To cook the lime-chili quinoa:
- Bring the quinoa and chicken stock to a boil over high heat.
- Reduce the heat to medium and stir in the lime zest.
- Cover with a tight-fitting lid and simmer until the quinoa is cooked.
- Allow to cool slightly, then add the cayenne pepper and lime juice, and fluff with a fork to mix the seasoning.
- To assemble:
- Top the quinoa with the tuna slices and serve.

Per serving: Calories: 279 Protein: 23g Carbs: 33g Fiber: 4g Sugar: 2g Fat: 4g

Seared Salmon Fillets and Sautéed Leeks

SERVES: 2 / PREP TIME: 5 MINUTES / COOK TIME: 30 MINUTES

Leeks are an excellent source of vitamins and antioxidants, and taste great when slowly sautéed on a medium-low heat.

2 x 4oz. salmon fillets, skinless and boneless
Olive oil cooking spray
1.5 cups chopped leeks
Juice of 1 lemon

- Preheat the oven to 400°F.
- Arrange the salmon fillets on aluminum foil sheets, and bake for 20 to 30 minutes until the salmon is cooked through.
- Meanwhile, lightly spray a nonstick pan with olive oil cooking spray and heat over high heat.
- Add the chopped leeks, and sauté for 1 minute.
- Lower the heat to low, and allow the leeks to cook, stirring occasionally, until they are softened. The leeks can cook for the duration that the salmons are in the oven, but be sure to cook on low, and stir occasionally to prevent the leeks from sticking to the pan or charring.
- To serve:
- Top the salmon fillets with the leeks and drizzle generously with the lemon juice.

Hint: Cook up a batch of sautéed leeks and keep chilled until ready to serve. Top over sashimi-quality salmon slices, or salads for added vitamins to your meal.

Per serving: Calories: 212 Protein: 29g Carbs: 11g Fiber: 1g Sugar: 3g Fat: 5g

Salmon and Sweet Corn Soup

SERVES: 2 / PREP TIME: 5 MINUTES / COOK TIME: 20 MINUTES

An easy to prepare soup that is both nutritious and tasty.

---

2 cups vegetable stock
1 tbsp. fresh thyme
6 oz. salmon fillets, skinless and boneless
1 cup yellow corn kernels
Freshly ground black pepper

- In a soup pot, bring the fish stock and fresh thyme to the boil over high heat.
- Reduce the heat, and add the salmon fillets.
- Cover the pot with a lid, and continue simmering until the fish is cooked (12 minutes or according to package directions).
- Add the corn kernels, and bring to a boil again.
- Serve hot, and season with freshly ground black pepper.

Per serving: Calories: 220 Protein: 26g Carbs: 20g Fiber: 2g Sugar: 5g Fat: 5g

Seared Teriyaki Salmon with a Black Bean and Green Mango Salad

SERVES: 2 / PREP TIME: 10 MINUTES / COOK TIME: 15 MINUTES

Ginger-seared salmon paired with a tangy, raw mango salad.

1/4 cup canned black beans
1/4 chopped shallots
1 tbsp. fresh cilantro, chopped
Juice from 1/2 lemon
1/2 green mango, sliced
1 tbsp. apple cider vinegar
1 tbsp. reduced sodium teriyaki sauce

1 tsp. grated ginger
5 oz. salmon fillet, skinless and boneless
Olive oil cooking spray

- To make the black bean and mango salad:
- Combine the black beans, shallots, fresh cilantro, lemon juice, sliced green mango, and apple cider vinegar in a salad bowl, and chill until ready to serve.
- Combine the teriyaki sauce with the grated ginger, and rub into the salmon fillets.
- Lightly spray a nonstick pan with the cooking spray, and heat over medium heat.
- Sear the salmon fillets for 5 to 6 minutes on each side, until they are cooked through.
- Serve hot with the chilled black beans and green mango salad.

Per serving: Calories: 208 Protein: 19g Carbs: 24g Fiber: 5g Sugar: 12g Fat: 5g

Tuna and Veggie Fritters

SERVES: 2 / PREP TIME: 10 MINUTES / COOK TIME: 8 MINUTES

A great way to use easily available canned tuna for adding flavor to vegetable fritters.

1 tbsp. flaxseed meal
2 1/2 tbsp. water
1/4 cup grated zucchini
1/4 cup grated potatoes
1/4 cup grated carrots
1 tbsp. chopped chives
4 oz. canned tuna in water
1/4 tsp. lemon juice
1 tbsp. brown rice flour

- Combine the flaxseed meal with the water, and let it rest until it thickens.
- Combine the vegetables, tuna, and lemon juice, and form fritters of desired size with your hands.
- Preheat the Airfryer to 350°F.
- Lightly dredge the fritters with the flax egg mixed earlier, and dust with the brown rice flour.
- Arrange the fritters in the Airfryer Basket, and set the timer for 8 minutes, or until the fritters are cooked through, flipping them over halfway during the cooking time to allow for even cooking.

Hint: The fritters can also be pan-fried or baked in the oven for the same amount of time or until golden brown and hot through.

Per serving: Calories: 109 Protein: 13g Carbs: 9g Fiber: 3g Sugar: 1g Fat: 3g

Potato and Cod Stew

SERVES: 2 / PREP TIME: 5 MINUTES / COOK TIME: 25 MINUTES

This delicious stew is the perfect way to warm up on a cold Winter's night.

---

1 cup fish stock
1/2 cup water
1 bay leaf
1/2 tsp. ground turmeric
1/2 tsp. paprika
1 tsp. dried oregano
1 medium potato, diced

2 beef tomatoes, diced
6 oz. cod fillets, boneless and skinless
1 tbsp. fresh parsley

- Bring the fish stock and water to the boil in a medium pot over high heat.
- Add the bay leaf, ground turmeric, paprika, dried oregano, potato, and beef tomatoes to the soup, and simmer on medium-low.
- Add the cod fillets to the soup, and continue to simmer until the fish is cooked through (about 15 minutes).
- If a thicker stew is preferred, continue to simmer uncovered until the stew is reduced.
- Top with the fresh parsley to serve.

Per serving: Calories: 186 Protein: 19g Carbs: 26g Fiber: 4g Sugar: 6g Fat: 1g

Baked Lemon and Parsley-Crusted Sea Bass

SERVES: 2 / PREP TIME: 10 MINUTES / COOK TIME: 20 MINUTES

A healthy sea bass dish baked in freshly made breadcrumbs.

1/2 slice whole wheat bread, toasted and crumbled into breadcrumbs
1 tbsp. fresh parsley, chopped
Juice of 1/2 lemon
2x 6oz. sea bass fillets

- Preheat the oven to 425°F.
- Combine the breadcrumbs, parsley, and lemon juice, and coat the top of the sea bass fillets with the breadcrumbs.
- Lay the sea bass fillets on aluminum foil pieces and bake for 20 minutes or until the fish is cooked through.
- Serve hot and slice in half if using one fillet.
- Accompany with your favorite vegetables or side salad.

Per serving: Calories: 71 Protein: 15g Carbs: 1g Fiber: 0g Sugar: 0g Fat: 1g

Thai-Style Cod en Papillote

SERVES: 4 / PREP TIME: 5 MINUTES / COOK TIME: 10 MINUTES

Lightly spiced and fragrant.

---

2 stalks lemongrass, bruised and chopped
1/4 cup ginger root, sliced
1/2 cup snow peas
1 tbsp. fresh cilantro
2 x 6oz. cod fillets
2 tbsp. fish sauce

Juice of 1 lime

- Preheat the oven to 425°F.
- Cut two pieces of parchment paper large enough to form parcels for the cod.
- In the center of each parchment parcel, arrange the lemongrass, ginger, snow peas, and fresh cilantro.
- Place the cod fillets on top of the vegetables.
- Season the cod with the fish sauce and lime juice.
- Fold the parchment paper to enclose the cod fillets loosely.
- Bake for 10 minutes, and allow the packets to cool for about 5 minutes before opening and serving with all the delicious juices.

Per serving: Calories: 96 Protein: 16g Carbs: 6g Fiber: 1g Sugar: 2g Fat: 1g

Chinese-Style Halibut with Wild Rice and Bok Choy

SERVES: 3 / PREP TIME: 5 MINUTES / COOK TIME: 20 MINUTES

A one-pot dish, freshly steamed and delicious.

1/2 cup bok choy
6 oz. halibut fillet
1 tbsp. reduced sodium soy sauce
1 tsp. sesame oil
4 scallion stems, chopped
1 tbsp. fresh cilantro leaves
1 cup cooked wild rice

- On a flat bowl that can fit the steamer snugly, arrange the bok choy on the sides of the plate, and the halibut fillets in the center of the plate.
- Combine the soy sauce, sesame oil, scallions, and cilantro leaves and drizzle over the halibut fillets.
- Steam for 15 to 20 minutes or until the fish is cooked through.
- Flake the halibut with a knife and fork.
- Spoon the sauce and the flaked halibut over the wild rice to serve.

Hint: Wild rice is a good alternative to white rice for a weight loss diet. Cook up a batch, and store in the fridge until ready to serve. Use a double-rack steamer so that the rice can be reheated while the fish and vegetables are cooking.

Per serving: Calories: 212 Protein: 28g Carbs: 13g Fiber: 1g Sugar: 1g Fat: 5g

Tilapia, Garlic, and Tomato Bake

SERVES: 2 / PREP TIME: 5 MINUTES / COOK TIME: 25 MINUTES

Simply add to an oven dish and allow to cook. Great when you're too tired to be standing by the stove for ages.

Olive oil cooking spray
1 cup cherry tomatoes, halved
2 cloves garlic
1 tbsp. balsamic vinegar
2x 4oz. tilapia fillets
2 tbsp. fresh basil, shredded

- Preheat the oven to 425°F.
- Lightly spray an ovenproof dish with olive oil cooking spray, and arrange the cherry tomatoes and garlic cloves on the dish.
- Drizzle the balsamic vinegar over the tomatoes.
- Roast the tomatoes and garlic for 15 minutes.
- Add the fish fillets on top of the tomato juices, and bake for another 10 minutes, or until the fish is cooked through.
- Top with the fresh basil to serve.

Per serving: Calories: 131 Protein: 22g Carbs: 5g Fiber: 1g Sugar: 3g Fat: 2g

BBQ Sole Fillets with Parsley, Mint, and Tomato Salsa

SERVES: 4 / PREP TIME: 35 MINUTES / COOK TIME: NA

Rather than enjoy this salsa as a side, the BBQ sole fillets are flaked and added to the salsa, rather like the bulghar in a tabbouleh.

Juice of 2 lemons
1 beef tomato, finely diced
2 tbsp. chopped shallots
2 cups chopped parsley
1 cup chopped mint
4 x sole fillets, barbecued or broiled

- To make the parsley, mint, and tomato salsa:
- Combine the lemon juice, diced tomatoes, chopped shallots, chopped parsley, and chopped mint in a bowl, and chill for at least 30 minutes, or until ready to serve.
- Flake the barbecued sole fillets and add to the salsa just before serving.

Per serving: Calories: 133 Protein: 20g Carbs: 7g Fiber: 2g Sugar: 2g Fat: 3g

Grilled Cod with Sweet Potato Mash and Cumin Yogurt

SERVES: 2 / PREP TIME: 10 MINUTES / COOK TIME: 30 MINUTES

Ideal for a hot day, this dish makes a filling yet refreshing meal.

Olive oil cooking spray
2x 6 oz. cod fillets
2 cups cubed sweet potatoes
1/2 cup low fat plain yogurt
1 tsp. ground cumin

- Preheat the oven to 350°F.
- Lightly spray an ovenproof dish with cooking spray, and arrange the cod fillets on the dish.
- Bake for 20 to 30 minutes, or until the fish is cooked through.
- While the fish is cooking, cook the sweet potatoes in a pot of boiling water, until they are softened.
- Drain from the water, and mash the sweet potatoes.
- Season the yogurt with ground cumin.
- To serve, arrange the cod on the sweet potato mash, and top with the cumin yogurt.

Hint: The sweet potato mash can be baked for 15 to 20 minutes to achieve a crispier texture, and thus, a delicious contrast to the cool cumin yogurt.

Per serving: Calories: 268 Protein: 35g Carbs: 25g Fiber: 3gSugar: 11g Fat: 3g

Low Fat Fish Tacos with Kale Leaves

SERVES: 2 / PREP TIME: 10 MINUTES / COOK TIME: 15 MINUTES

A great way to add the superfood kale to an all-time favorite.

1/4 cup chopped scallions
1/4 cup chopped cilantro
2 tbsp. fat free sour cream
Juice of 1 lime
1/2 clove garlic, minced
6 oz. cod (or other white fish fillets), skinless and boneless, cubed
1 tsp. ground cumin
1 tsp. coriander seeds
1/2 tsp. paprika
1/2 tsp. red pepper flakes
2 small whole wheat tortillas
1 cup kale leaves, shredded

- To make the sauce:
- Combine the chopped scallions, cilantro, sour cream, lime juice, and minced garlic in a bowl, and set aside.
- Season the fish fillet cubes with the ground cumin, coriander seeds, paprika, and red pepper flakes.
- Cook the fish under a hot broiler for 4 to 5 minutes on each side, or until the fish is thoroughly cooked through.
- Remove and place to one side.
- When the fish has slightly cooled, mix with the sauce until well combined.
- Gently toast the tortillas under the broiler for 1-2 minutes.
- To assemble, spoon the fish onto the tortillas, and top with the shredded kale leaves.

Per serving: Calories: 227 Protein: 21g Carbs: 27g Fiber: 6g Sugar: 3g Fat: 5g

VEGETARIAN

Provençal Ratatouille

SERVES: 2 / PREP TIME: 5 MINUTES / COOK TIME: 35 MINUTES

This is a quick go-to vegetable stew with a Provençal flavor.

Olive oil cooking spray
2 tbsp. onions, chopped
1 clove garlic, minced
1/2 cup pumpkin, diced
2 medium carrots, diced
1 large turnip, diced
1 cup zucchinis, sliced

2 beef tomatoes, chopped
1 tsp. dried Herbs de Provence
1 cup water
1 cup baby spinach leaves

- Spray a large pan with the cooking spray and heat over medium heat.
- Add the onions, garlic, pumpkin, carrots, turnip, and zucchini, and cook for 5 minutes or until the vegetables are starting to soften.
- Add in the chopped tomatoes and dried herbs, and simmer until thickened, stirring frequently to prevent the vegetables from burning, for about 15 minutes.
- Add the water, and simmer for another 15 to 20 minutes until the sauce is reduced, and the vegetables are cooked.
- Top with the baby spinach leaves to serve.

Hint: If you've got a bit longer for cooking - sauté each vegetable separately, and use vegetable stock in the place of water for the tomato base. Only mix the cooked vegetables together when the tomato base is made, bring to a boil, and remove from the heat. Allow the ratatouille to rest so that the flavors can blend well for a hearty dish.

Per serving: Calories: 133 Protein: 7g Carbs: 29g Fiber: 9g Sugar: 14g Fat: 1g

Veggie Chili

SERVES: 4 / PREP TIME: 10 MINUTES / COOK TIME: 30 MINUTES

A great companion to a meat dish, low-carb tortillas, or as a topping for a crispy green salad.

Olive oil cooking spray
2 tbsp. chopped onions
1 cup diced red peppers
1 clove garlic, minced
1/2 cup diced winter squash
1 cup cherry tomatoes, halved
1 cup reduced sodium canned tomatoes
1/2 cup dark red, reduced sodium canned kidney beans (liquid reserved)
1 cup reduced sodium canned black beans (liquid reserved)
1 jalapeño pepper, sliced
2 tsp. lime juice

- Spray the cooking spray into a nonstick pan, and heat on medium heat.
- Add the onions, red peppers, garlic, and squash to the pan.
- Cover the pan, reduce the heat to low, and cook for 10 minutes.
- Mix in the cherry tomatoes, canned tomatoes, beans, jalapeño pepper, and lime juice.
- Simmer for 20 minutes.
- Serve hot.

Hint: The chili becomes a darker red when cooked. The juice from the cherry tomatoes gives the dish a rich flavor. If more liquid is required, use the reserved liquids from the beans, or water. Season with a little brown sugar to sweeten the chili, or cayenne pepper to spice it up.

Per serving: Calories: 133 Protein: 6g Carbs: 24g Fiber: 5g Sugar: 4g Fat: 0g

Crunchy Super Salad

SERVES: 2 / PREP TIME: 10 MINUTES / COOK TIME: NA

This crunchy salad can be served warm or cold, and is very tasty.

---

1 tsp. dry mustard
1 tbsp. lemon juice
1/4 cup apple cider vinegar
2 tbsp. mint leaves
5 cherry tomatoes, stems removed
2 cups zucchini noodles
1/2 carrot, peeled and grated

1/2 yellow pepper, thinly sliced
1/4 cup cooked red quinoa
Freshly ground black pepper

- To make the dressing:
- Blend the mustard, lemon juice, apple cider vinegar, mint leaves, and cherry tomatoes in a food processor.
- Transfer to a bowl, and keep chilled until ready to serve.
- Toss together the zucchini noodles, carrots, and pepper with the dressing.
- To serve:
- Top the zucchini noodles with the cooked quinoa, and season with freshly ground black pepper.

Hint: When making zucchini noodles, use a spiralizer and stop when you reach the seeds of the zucchini, as the shape will not hold from the seedy flesh. Zucchini noodles can be eaten raw, or blanched in boiling water for 1-2 minutes for a warm dish.

Per serving: Calories: 118 Protein: 4g Carbs: 23g Fiber: 2g   Sugar: 2g Fat: 1g

Refreshing Zucchini and Parsley Noodles

SERVES: 2 / PREP TIME: 30 MINUTES / COOK TIME: NA

Every spoonful is a crunchy and juicy delight, and is perfect for hot, summer picnics.

Juice of 1 lemon
2 beef tomatoes, diced
1 cup fresh parsley, chopped
1 clove garlic, minced
1 tbsp. chopped shallots
3 cups zucchini noodles

- To make the dressing:
- Mix the lemon juice, beef tomatoes, fresh parsley, garlic, and shallots in a bowl, and allow to rest for at least 30 minutes for the flavors to blend.
- Toss in the cold zucchini noodles, and serve.

Hint: When making zucchini noodles, use a spiralizer and stop when you reach the seeds of the zucchini, as the shape will not hold from the seedy flesh. Zucchini noodles can be eaten raw, or blanched in boiling water for 1-2 minutes for a warm dish.

Per serving: Calories: 91 Protein: 7g Carbs: 18g Fiber: 3g Sugar: 10g Fat: 1g

Airfried Carrot and Zucchini Fritters

SERVES: 2 / PREP TIME: 15 MINUTES / COOK TIME: 10 MINUTES

Airfrying reduces the need for oil, and a flax egg replaces a regular egg, making this a delicious and healthy fritter.

---

1 tsp. salt
1 large zucchini, grated
1 tbsp. flax meal
2 1/2 tbsp. water
1 large clove of garlic, minced
1 cup grated carrots

- Add the salt to the grated zucchinis, and allow to rest for 5 to 10 minutes, so that the salt can draw out the excess water from the zucchinis. Rinse well, and drain from the water. Pat them dry with a kitchen towel and set aside.
- Preheat the Airfryer to 350°F.
- To make the flax egg, mix the flax meal with water and allow to rest until it thickens.
- Combine the zucchini, carrots, garlic, and flax egg, and form patties of desired size.
- Arrange the patties in the Airfryer Basket, and set the timer for 10 minutes. Halfway through the cooking time, flip the fritters over to allow even cooking.

Hint: Any combination of vegetables that can hold their shape when grated can be used to make vegetable fritters.

Hint: If you don't have an airfryer, use olive oil cooking spray and a hot skillet to sauté the fritters for 4-5 minutes on each side until golden brown and crispy, and hot all the way through.

Per serving: Calories: 81 Protein: 4g   Carbs: 14g Fiber: 5g Sugar: 6g Fat: 2g

Roasted Fennel with Apple Cider Glaze

SERVES: 2 / PREP TIME: 10 MINUTES / COOK TIME: 45 MINUTES

Slow roasted and caramelized.

---

1 cup reduced sugar apple cider
1 tsp. fennel seeds
Olive oil cooking spray
2 cups sliced fennel bulbs

- Preheat the oven to 325°F.
- Combine the apple cider and fennel seeds in a saucepan, and simmer over low heat until the liquid has thickened to a glaze, and reduced by half.
- Strain the glaze from the seeds.
- Lightly spray an ovenproof dish with cooking spray, and arrange the sliced fennel in the dish.
- Brush the fennel with the glaze.
- Roast for 30 to 45 minutes, re-coating with the glaze every 10 to 15 minutes.
- The fennels can be slow-roasted until they are tender and caramelized.

Hint: We have used fennel seeds for this recipe to enhance the taste of the fennel bulbs, but it can work well with other fresh or dried herbs.

Per serving: Calories: 79 Protein: 1g Carbs: 11g Fiber: 3g Sugar: 6g Fat: 0g

Truffle Cauliflower Bake

SERVES: 2 / PREP TIME: 5 MINUTES / COOK TIME: 40 MINUTES

Indulge in a little truffle luxury.

Olive oil cooking spray, (white truffle flavored if possible)
2 cups cauliflower florets
1 clove garlic, minced
1 cup cherry tomatoes, halved
1/2 tsp. truffle salt
Freshly ground black pepper

- Preheat oven to 350°F.
- Lightly spray an ovenproof serving dish with the white truffle flavored olive oil cooking spray.
- Toss the cauliflower florets with the minced garlic and cherry tomatoes, and arrange them evenly in the base of the dish.
- Season with the truffle salt and freshly ground black pepper, and bake for 30 to 40 minutes, or until the cauliflower florets are fork-tender.

Hint: The cauliflower will cook to a crispy texture without any liquids, but if desired, a little liquid can be added to the dish to steam them.

Hint: If you can't find truffle oil and truffle salt, substitute for garlic oil and salt.

Per serving: Calories: 45 Protein: 3g Carbs: 7g Fiber: 4g Sugar: 4g Fat: 0g

Lime-Roasted Eggplants

SERVES: 2 / PREP TIME: 15 MINUTES / COOK TIME: 30 MINUTES

Perfect as a side for a chicken or fish dish, or alone with a side salad.

---

2 tsp. salt
3 cups cubed eggplants
1/4 cup lime juice
Olive oil cooking spray

- Preheat the oven to 350°F.
- Sprinkle the salt on the cubed eggplants, and allow to rest for 10 minutes to draw out excess water.
- Rinse the eggplants thoroughly to remove the salt, and pat dry with a clean kitchen towel.
- Toss the eggplant cubes in the lime juice.
- Lightly spray an ovenproof dish with the cooking spray, and arrange the eggplant cubes in the base of the dish.
- Bake for 25 to 30 minutes, or until the eggplants are cooked through and soft.

Hint: This dish can also be cooked in a nonstick pan over medium heat. Lightly spray the pan with the cooking spray, and add the eggplants to the pan. Cook until the eggplants are done, and stir frequently to ensure that they do not burn.

Per serving: Calories: 39 Protein: 1g   Carbs: 10g Fiber: 4g Sugar: 5g Fat: 0g

Grilled Tomatoes with Black Garlic Spread

SERVES: 2 / PREP TIME: 5 MINUTES / COOK TIME: 40 MINUTES

Black garlic gives an earthiness and depth to a tangy, grilled tomato dish.

---

3 bulbs black garlic (or try white garlic/wild garlic if you can't find black garlic)
3 beef tomatoes

- Preheat the oven to 350°F.
- Cut the tops off the black garlic bulbs so that the tops of the cloves are exposed. Place the bulbs on a small ovenproof dish.
- Slice the beef tomatoes each into four slices, and arrange them on an ovenproof dish.
- Bake the tomatoes and the garlic bulbs in the oven for 35 to 40 minutes.
- When done, spread the soft flesh of the garlic on top of the tomato slices to serve.

Hint: To get a fuller flavor from the grilled tomatoes, remove the pulps and seeds from the tomato slices, and flavor them generously with dried herbs. Grill the tomatoes for 25 minutes until they become slightly crisp, then spoon over the reserved seeds and pulps into the tomato cavities. Grill for another 20 minutes until the juices are bubbling. To serve, spread the black garlic mash in the centre of a serving plate, and top with the grilled tomatoes. This will give a great texture and different layers of flavors for the dish.

Per serving: Calories: 90 Protein: 6g Carbs: 18g Fiber: 0g Sugar: 11g Fat: 0g

Tomato and Arugula Egg White Scramble

SERVES: 2 / PREP TIME: 5 MINUTES / COOK TIME: 10 MINUTES

A healthy alternative to regular scrambled eggs.

```
Olive oil cooking spray
1 large onion, chopped
2 beef tomatoes, diced
3 large egg whites, whisked
1 cup arugula leaves, shredded
```

- Lightly spray a nonstick pan with the cooking spray, and heat over medium heat.
- Add the chopped onions, and sauté until they become translucent.
- Add the diced tomatoes, and cook until the tomatoes have released their liquids, about three minutes.
- Add the whisked egg whites, and allow to set for a couple of minutes.
- Add the arugula leaves, and scramble the egg whites so that the ingredients are well combined.

Hint: If desired, serve the arugula leaves topped over the scrambled eggs after cooking.

Per serving: Calories: 92 Protein: 10g Carbs: 14g Fiber: 1g Sugar: 8g Fat: 1g

Sunshine Pie

SERVES: 6 / PREP TIME: 10 MINUTES / COOK TIME: 1 HOUR

This dish uses bright yellow spaghetti squash and is sure to bring a smile to the dinner table.

1.5 lb spaghetti squash
1 tsp. olive oil
1 clove garlic, minced
1 tbsp. chopped onions
1/2 cup sliced mushrooms
1/4 cup chopped red peppers
1 cup canned chopped tomatoes
1 tsp. dried oregano
1 cup shredded low fat mozzarella cheese

- Preheat the oven to 375°F.
- To prepare the spaghetti squash:
- Half the squash and discard its seeds.
- Place each half face down in a 9x13-inch baking dish. Cover and bake for 30-40 minutes until soft.
- Remove and allow to cool. When cool enough to handle, scrape out the flesh of the squash, and mash to a smooth consistency.
- Meanwhile, prepare the filling:
- Heat the olive oil in a large saucepan over medium heat. Add the garlic and onions, and cook for 2 minutes, stirring frequently. Add the mushrooms, bell peppers, chopped tomatoes, and dried oregano to the pan, and bring to a boil.
- Reduce the heat, and simmer for 15 to 20 minutes, until the sauce has thickened, stirring occasionally.
- To assemble: Transfer the tomato filling into an ovenproof serving dish. Top with the squash, and then the mozzarella cheese.
- Bake for 25 minutes or until lightly browned. Let cool for 5 minutes before serving.

Hint: Spaghetti squash can also be used to substitute mashed potatoes in a cottage pie.

Per serving: Calories: 81 Protein: 6g Carbs: 4g Fiber: 1g Sugar: 2g Fat: 5g

Kale Fruit Salad

SERVES: 2 / PREP TIME: 15 MINUTES / COOK TIME: NA

A refreshing, juicy, and crunchy salad, with tangerine for a sweet boost!

---

1 small tangerine, juiced
3 cups baby kale leaves, shredded
1/2 cup pears, thinly sliced

- Toss together the tangerine juice, baby kale leaves, and pears in a salad bowl.
- Allow to chill for 15 minutes for the flavors to blend.
- Optional: Dress with a little apple cider vinegar to balance out the sweet fruit.

Hint: Choose the juiciest pears and tangerines for this dish to be really sweet and refreshing.

Per serving: Calories: 82 Protein: 4g Carbs: 19g Fiber: 5g Sugar: 10gn Fat: 1g

Savory Tofu

SERVES: 2 / PREP TIME: 10 MINUTES / COOK TIME: 20 MINUTES

Use this mix of Asian seasoning to enhance the taste of tofu, while enjoying the nutritional benefits it has to offer.

---

1 tsp. minced ginger
1 tbsp. oyster sauce
1 tbsp. reduced sodium soy sauce
1 tsp. white pepper
1/4 tbsp. pure sesame oil
3 1/2 oz. extra firm, high-protein, low fat tofu

3 tbsp. chopped scallions

- To make the seasoning:
- Combine the minced ginger, oyster sauce, soy sauce, white pepper, and sesame oil in a bowl.
- Rinse the tofu, and pat dry with a kitchen towel.
- Arrange on a heat-proof steaming bowl, and drizzle the seasoning over the tofu.
- Steam the tofu for 15 to 20 minutes until done, and spoon over the seasoning several times throughout the cooking time.
- Alternatively, heat a little sesame oil in a screaming hot pan and add the tofu for 3-4 minutes until crispy and brown.
- Top with the chopped scallions to serve.

Hint: If using a smooth silky tofu that can be eaten raw, remove the tofu from the package and pat dry any excess water. Place the tofu in a bowl. Coat the tofu with the seasoning, and chopped scallions. Chill until ready to serve.

Per serving: Calories: 117 Protein: 10g Carbs: 12g Fiber: 0g Sugar: 1g Fat: 5g

Baked Sweet Cabbage

SERVES: 2 / PREP TIME: 10 MINUTES / COOK TIME: 55 MINUTES

A filling and nourishing dish for a cold day or a lovely side dish for a barbecue.

---

2 large cabbage leaves
1 tsp. olive oil
1/2 medium onion, diced
1 small carrot, grated
1 tsp. dried oregano
1 cup canned tomatoes

- Preheat oven to 350°F.
- Bring a pot of water to the boil.
- Wash the cabbage leaves and blanch them in the hot water for 30 seconds. Pat dry, and set aside.
- Heat the olive oil in a nonstick pan over medium heat.
- Add the onions, carrots, and dried oregano, stirring for a few minutes until the vegetables are slightly soft and caramelised.
- Divide the vegetable mixture into the center of each cabbage leaf, and roll up to seal the vegetables.
- Arrange the cabbage rolls, seam sides down, in a small baking dish.
- Top with the canned tomatoes, and bake for 35 to 40 minutes.
- Allow to cool for 5 to 10 minutes before serving.

Hint: If desired, omit the canned tomatoes, and steam the cabbage rolls in 1/2 cup vegetable stock in a steamer for 20 to 25 minutes. For a non-vegetarian take, some minced chicken can be added to the vegetables, and replace the vegetable stock with chicken stock.

Per serving: Calories: 111 Protein: 2g   Carbs: 11g Fiber: 6g Sugar: 6g Fat: 2g

High-Protein Scrambled Eggs

SERVES: 2 / PREP TIME: 5 MINUTES / COOK TIME: 10 MINUTES

A perfect recipe for a high-protein, low-carb, quick meal.

Olive oil cooking spray
1 tbsp. chopped onions
1 large egg white
1 egg
1/4 tsp. cayenne pepper
1/8 tsp. ground nutmeg
1 tbsp. low fat cottage cheese

1/2 cup diced low fat cheddar cheese
2 cups baby spinach leaves

- Lightly spray a nonstick pan with the cooking spray.
- Add the chopped onions, and cook until they are translucent.
- Whisk together the egg white, egg, cayenne pepper, and ground nutmeg, and pour into the pan.
- When the eggs begin to set, add the cottage and cheddar cheeses, and cook until your desired consistency and texture - around 4-5 minutes for runny, 5-6 for soft and 7-8 for harder eggs.
- Top with the baby spinach leaves to serve.
- You can allow the spinach to wilt and then stir through the eggs if desired.

Per serving: Calories: 127 Protein: 17g Carbs: 3g Fiber: 1g Sugar: 1g Fat: 5g

Peppered and Herbed Egg Muffins

SERVES: 12 MUFFINS / PREP TIME: 5 MINUTES / COOK TIME: 25 MINUTES

An easy-to-make dish, great for brunches and picnics.

Olive oil cooking spray
6 large eggs
3/4 cup low fat Swiss cheese, shredded
1/2 cup skim milk
4 oz. diced red peppers
2 tbsp. chopped chives
2 tbsp. chopped fresh parsley

- Preheat oven to 350°F, and spray a 12-cup muffin tin with the cooking spray.
- Combine the eggs, 1/2 cup shredded cheese, the skim milk, red peppers, chopped chives, and chopped parsley in a bowl.
- Divide the batter into the muffin cups, and top with the remaining shredded cheese.
- Bake for 20 to 25 minutes, or until the eggs are cooked to desired consistency.

Hint: For greater flavor, use roasted red peppers in the place of raw red peppers, or use up any leftover carrots and zucchinis, and finely grate them for the recipe.

Per muffin serving: Calories: 58 Protein: 6g Carbs: 2g Fiber: 0g Sugar: 1g Fat: 3g

Tomato and Herb Pizettes

SERVES: 5 / PREP TIME: 5 MINUTES / COOK TIME: 25 MINUTES

Healthy miniature versions of a classic indulgence.

---

12 cherry tomatoes, halved
¼ tsp. garlic powder
1 tsp. dried oregano
6 light multigrain English muffins, sliced in half
1 cup finely sliced green pepper
4 oz. fat free mozzarella cheese, sliced into thin disks
¼ cup fresh basil, chopped
2 tsp. balsamic vinegar

- Preheat the oven to 400°F.
- Line a baking sheet with parchment paper.
- Layer the baking sheet with the tomato halves.
- Evenly sprinkle on the garlic powder and oregano.
- Give the tomatoes a spray with cooking oil.
- Roast in the oven until the tomato skins begin to split (about 10 minutes).
- Take the tray out and set it aside.
- Line another baking sheet with parchment paper.
- Place the English muffin halves on the baking sheets, cut-side up.
- Divide the pepper, cheese, and roasted tomatoes onto the muffins.
- Finally sprinkle the basil evenly over all 12 pizzas.
- Bake the pizzas in the oven for 10-12 minutes, or until the cheese is all melted and gooey.
- Drizzle with balsamic vinegar before serving.

Per serving: Calories: 191 Protein: 14g Carbs: 33g Fiber: 6g Sugar: 8g Fat: 2g

Spinach and Mozzarella Bake

SERVES: 4 / PREP TIME: 10 MINUTES / COOK TIME: 30 MINUTES

Cheesy, delicious and a great vegetarian dinner option. Serve with a leafy salad.

½ cup non fat mozzarella cheese
2 cups fresh spinach, cooked and drained
1 eggplant, diced
1 zucchini, diced
½ cup tomato paste
½ cup frozen peas

1 tbsp. dried basil
1 tbsp. low fat parmesan/cheddar cheese

- Preheat your oven to 375°F.
- In a bowl, mix the mozzarella and spinach together.
- In another bowl, mix the eggplant, zucchini and ½ the tomato paste.
- Save the rest of the paste for later.
- You'll need a lasagna dish for the next part.
- Spoon the mozzarella and spinach mixture into the base.
- Spoon the vegetable mixture in to form the next layer.
- Cover with the reserved paste.
- Sprinkle with the basil and hard cheese.
- Cook for 30 minutes or until golden brown and bubbly.
- Remove from the oven and slice into portions.
- Spoon onto your plates and enjoy!

Per serving: Calories: 135 Protein: 13g Carbs: 24g Fiber: 10g Sugar: 12g Fat: 1g

Luxurious Cauliflower Cheese

SERVES: 5 / PREP TIME: 5 MINUTES / COOK TIME: 35 MINUTES

An old family favorite - creamy and delicious.

---

1 cauliflower, trimmed and cut into florets
¾ cup low fat ricotta cheese
1 cup low fat plain yogurt
2 small eggs, beaten
1 clove garlic, crushed
1 tbsp. wholegrain or English mustard
1 tsp. dried parsley
1 cup grated fat-free hard cheese
A pinch of salt and freshly ground black pepper to taste

- Preheat the oven to 200°F.
- Cook the cauliflower in boiling water for 5-10 minutes until tender-crisp.
- Drain thoroughly in a colander.
- Mix the ricotta with the yogurt, eggs, garlic, mustard, parsley, 3/4 cup cheese and salt and pepper to taste.
- Fold the cauliflower into the cheesy mixture.
- Transfer to an ovenproof baking dish and sprinkle with the remaining cheese.
- Bake for about 25 minutes until golden and bubbly.
- Serve hot.

Hint: Sprinkle on some lightly baked whole wheat breadcrumbs for a crunchy topping.

Per serving: Calories: 160 Protein: 18g Carbs: 12g Fiber: 3g Sugar: 6g Fat: 5g

Fresh Chickpea Salad

SERVES: 2 / PREP TIME: 10 MINUTES / COOK TIME: NA

This salad tastes great with mint, lemon, and tangy olives.

3/4 cup canned chickpeas, drained
1 tbsp. olive oil
1 tbsp. balsamic vinegar
Juice of 1 lemon
2oz. low fat feta cheese, crumbled
12 cherry tomatoes, halved
1 small cucumber, deseeded and diced
1/2 green onion, finely sliced
18 pitted black olives, halved
A pinch of salt and freshly ground black pepper
1 tbsp. chopped fresh mint
1 tsp. chopped fresh oregano
2 cups washed raw spinach leaves

- Place the chickpeas in a fine sieve.
- Rinse with plenty of cold water, then leave to drain thoroughly.
- Mix the oil and vinegar with the lemon juice.
- Place the feta, tomatoes, cucumber, onion, and olives in a large mixing bowl with the chickpeas.
- Mix, cover, and leave to rest in the fridge for 20-30 minutes if possible.
- Season the chickpea mixture and add the mint and oregano.
- Top the spinach leaves with the chickpea salad and serve.

Per serving: Calories: 82 Protein: 3 Carbs: 8g Fiber: 2g Sugar: 3g Fat: 5g

POULTRY

One-Tray Chicken and Kale Bake

SERVES: 2 / PREP TIME: 5 MINUTES / COOK TIME: 45 MINUTES

A perfect recipe that can be prepared the night before, and put in the oven when it's time to eat!

Canola oil cooking spray
1/2 onion, cut into wedges
2x small chicken breasts, boneless and skinless
1 cup reduced sodium chicken stock
1 tbsp. chopped fresh thyme
2 cups chopped kale

- Preheat the oven to 350°F.
- Lightly spray an ovenproof dish with the canola oil spray, and arrange the onions and chicken breasts in the dish.
- Pour in the chicken stock, and add the chopped fresh thyme.
- Bake for 25 minutes in the oven.
- Flip the chicken breasts over, and arrange the kale in the dish.
- Bake for another 20 minutes until the chicken is cooked through, and the kale is tender.
- Serve hot.

Per serving: Calories: 174 Protein: 28g Carbs: 8g Fiber: 2g Sugar: 0g Fat: 4g

Zucchini Pasta with Ground Turkey and Fresh Peaches

SERVES: 2 / PREP TIME: 5 MINUTES / COOK TIME: 10 MINUTES

A lovely summer dish, perfect when peaches are in season. Use canned as a replacement the rest of the year.

Canola oil cooking spray
1 onion, chopped
1 clove garlic, minced
4 oz. lean ground turkey
3 cups zucchini noodles
1 medium carrot, peeled and grated
1 cup sliced peaches

- Lightly spray a nonstick pan with the canola cooking spray, and heat over medium heat.
- Add the onions, garlic, and ground turkey, and sauté until the turkey is cooked through - 10-12 minutes.
- Toss the zucchini noodles with the ground turkey, grated carrots, and sliced peaches.
- Allow to heat through or serve immediately.

Hint: For a vegetarian take, toss zucchini noodles with grated carrots, juicy peaches, juicy nectarines, and some blueberries.

Per serving: Calories: 144 Protein: 12g Carbs: 15g Fiber: 3g Sugar: 10g Fat: 5g

Slow Cooker Polenta and Turkey Curry

SERVES: 2 / PREP TIME: 5 MINUTES / COOK TIME: 6-7 HOURS SLOW COOKER

A great dish to pop into the slow cooker before heading off for the day; ready for a delicious dinner when you return.

6 oz. skinless and boneless turkey breasts, cubed
1/2 cup canned tomatoes
1 medium onion, chopped
2 tsp. fresh garlic, crushed
2 tsp. fresh ginger, crushed
3 tsp. cumin powder
3 tbsp. water
1 tsp. garam masala
1 tbsp. coriander seeds
1/2 cup precooked polenta/cornmeal, cubed
2 tbsp. chopped fresh cilantro

- Place all the ingredients, except the polenta and cilantro, into the slow cooker pot, and set on LOW for 6-7 hours.
- About 30 minutes before serving, add the cubed polenta into the slow cooker.
- Garnish with the fresh cilantro to serve.

Hint: If desired, precooked polenta can be airfried, and then topped over with the curry. The crispy texture with curry is delicious.

Per serving: Calories: 237 Protein: 22g Carbs: 33g Fiber: 5g Sugar: 4g Fat: 5g

Salt and Peppered Grilled Chicken

SERVES: 2 / PREP TIME: 10 MINUTES / COOK TIME: 25 MINUTES

This savory feel-good grilled chicken paired with a bitter-sweet salad, makes for a delightful dinner.

1 cup sliced pears
1 cup arugula leaves
2x small skinless, boneless chicken breasts
A pinch of sea salt and pepper, to season
Olive oil cooking spray

2 tbsp. lemon juice

- To make the arugula fruit salad:
- Combine the pears and arugula leaves in a small salad bowl, and chill until ready to serve.
- Generously season the chicken breasts with sea salt and black pepper.
- Lightly spray a nonstick grill pan with the cooking spray, and heat on medium-high.
- Place the chicken breasts in the grill pan, and sear on both sides until lightly browned.
- Cover the pan with a fitting lid, and reduce the heat to medium-low.
- Let the chicken cook for 10 to 15 minutes more, or until cooked through.
- To serve, drizzle the lemon juice over the grilled chicken, alongside the arugula salad.

Per serving: Calories: 170 Protein: 23g Carbs: 13g Fiber: 3g Sugar: 8g Fat: 3g

Grilled Chicken and Caprése Sandwich

SERVES: 2 / PREP TIME: 5 MINUTES / COOK TIME: NA

This recipe uses tofu to replace mozzarella in a traditional caprése. It is a fun to prepare, colorful snack. Tofu can often be used to substitute processed or fresh mozzarella in other Italian dishes for a weight loss diet.

2x small grilled chicken breasts, thickly sliced
2 beef tomatoes, thinly sliced
3 oz. firm precooked tofu, thinly sliced
2 tbsp. fresh basil, torn
2 tsp. balsamic vinegar

- Assemble sandwiches by using the chicken slices as the sandwich 'bread'.
- Begin with a thick slice of chicken, add some tomatoes and tofu, top with some fresh basil, and drizzle over a little balsamic vinegar.
- Top with another slice of chicken, and secure with a toothpick if necessary.

Hint: Consider purchasing family-value packs of chicken breasts, and grilling them over a free weekend. Chill them in ready to eat portions as toppings on salads, or for adding protein to soups.

Per serving: Calories: 187 Protein: 28g Carbs: 9g Fiber: 3g   Sugar: 6g Fat: 5g

Airfried Chicken Satay with Cucumber Salsa

SERVES: 2 / PREP TIME: 10 MINUTES / COOK TIME: 15 MINUTES

A nutty chicken dish, paired with a refreshing, tangy salad.

Olive oil cooking spray
6 oz. skinless, boneless chicken breasts, cubed
1/2 tbsp. smooth peanut butter
1 cucumber, diced
2 tbsp. chopped shallots
1 tbsp. apple cider vinegar

- Preheat the Airfryer to 350°F, and lightly coat the Airfryer Baking Pan with the cooking spray.
- Coat the chicken cubes with the peanut butter, and arrange them in the Airfryer Baking Pan.
- Place the pan in the Airfryer Basket, and set the timer for 15 minutes, or until the chicken is cooked through, giving the pan a shake halfway through the cooking time to allow for even cooking.
- While the chicken is cooking, make the cucumber salsa by combining the cucumber, shallots, and apple cider vinegar in a small bowl. Keep chilled until ready to serve.

Hint: If you don't have an airfryer, preheat the broiler to medium-high and layer the chicken cubes on an aluminum lined oven sheet. Place under the broiler for 10-15 minutes, turning half way through and ensuring they are completely cooked through before removing and placing to one side. Serve with the cucumber salsa.

Per serving: Calories: 181 Protein: 27g Carbs: 5g Fiber: 1g Sugar: 3g Fat: 6g

Hoisin Chicken Cabbage Wraps

SERVES: 2 / PREP TIME: 5 MINUTES / COOK TIME: 20 MINUTES

Sweet chicken rolled in crunchy, juicy cabbage.

Canola oil cooking spray
4 oz. canned bamboo shoots, drained and sliced
1 tsp. minced ginger
2 cloves garlic, minced
6 oz. lean ground chicken breast
1 tsp. hoisin sauce

1 tsp. reduced sodium soy sauce
1/2 tsp. toasted sesame oil
1 tsp. shaoxing cooking wine
1/4 cup scallions, chopped
1/2 cup (4 oz). canned water chestnuts, drained and diced
2 large iceberg lettuce leaves, washed and patted dry

- Lightly spray a nonstick wok with the cooking spray, and sauté the bamboo shoots, minced ginger, minced garlic, and ground chicken, for 10-15 minutes or until the chicken is cooked through.
- Season with the hoisin sauce, soy sauce, sesame oil, and cooking wine.
- Add the scallions to the wok.
- Stir well to combine, bring to a boil, and remove from the heat.
- Stir in the water chestnuts.
- Divide the chicken between the iceberg lettuce leaves.
- Roll the lettuce leaves to form wraps so that the chicken is enclosed, and secure with a toothpick if necessary.

Hint: To get a leaner ground chicken, consider purchasing lean chicken fillets, and processing them with a food processor yourself.

Per serving: Calories: 206 Protein: 27g Carbs: 11g Fiber: 2g Sugar: 4g Fat: 6g

Airfried Chicken Kebabs

SERVES: 2 / PREP TIME: 20 MINUTES / COOK TIME: 15 MINUTES

Use the Airfryer Double Layer Rack with Skewers to enjoy juicy chicken skewers.

---

6 oz. chicken breasts, cubed
1/2 tsp. muscovado sugar
1 tsp. grated lime zest
Juice of 1/2 lime
1/2 onion, cut into wedges
2 beef tomatoes, cut into wedges

- Marinate the chicken cubes with the sugar, lime zest, and lime juice for at least 20 minutes.
- Preheat the Airfryer to 350°F.
- Skewer the chicken, onions, and tomatoes on the Airfryer skewers, and place the rack into the Airfryer Basket.
- Set the timer for 15 minutes, or until the chicken is cooked through.

Hint: If you don't have an airfryer, preheat the broiler to medium-high and layer the chicken skewers on an aluminum lined oven sheet. Place under the broiler for 10-15 minutes, turning half way through and ensuring they are completely cooked through before removing and serving.

Hint: Skewer tofu, polenta, and peaches as delicious alternatives to tomatoes and onions with chicken skewers.

Per serving: Calories: 185 Protein: 27g Carbs: 12g Fiber: 3g Sugar: 7g Fat: 4g

Shredded Chicken and Berry Salad

SERVES: 2 / PREP TIME: 5 MINUTES / COOK TIME: NA

A summer delight of fresh, juicy superberries and nutritious chicken.

---

6 oz. grilled chicken, shredded
1 cup peeled and grated carrot
1/2 cup shredded cucumbers
1/2 cup blueberries
1/2 cup strawberries, stems removed, and halved

- Combine the chicken, carrots, cucumbers, and berries in a salad bowl.
- Chill until ready to serve.

Hint: This salad does not need a dressing as every bite into the juicy vegetables and fruits will suffice. Serve with an iced, homemade, unsweetened tea topped with mint leaves, and enjoy the summer feeling light, slim, and healthy.

Per serving: Calories: 193 Protein: 27g Carbs: 14g Fiber: 3g Sugar: 8g Fat: 4g

Marinated Paprika Chicken

SERVES: 2 / PREP TIME: OVERNIGHT / COOK TIME: 20 MINUTES

A simple yet tasty marinated chicken dish, ready for the oven, the airfryer, the grill, or the BBQ.

2x small skinless chicken breasts
2 tsp. smoked paprika
1 tsp. ground cumin
1 tsp. ground ginger
Juice of 1 lemon
A pinch of salt and pepper, to taste

- Score 2-3 slits into the chicken breasts.
- Combine the smoked paprika, ground cumin, ground ginger, lemon juice, salt, and pepper, and rub the chicken evenly with the mixture, being sure to rub into the incisions.
- Refrigerate in an airtight container over night.
- Preheat the broiler or barbecue to medium-high when ready to cook.
- Place chicken breasts on an ovenproof sheet and broil for 6-8 minutes on each side.
- Ensure the chicken is thoroughly cooked through in its thickest part by inserting a sharp knife and ensuring liquids come out clear and there is no pink meat in the center.
- Serve with your choice of side salad.

Hint: The airfryer and fan-forced oven circulates the hot air around the chicken to cook it evenly. When using a grill or a BBQ, consider covering the chicken with a lid, and first searing on hot heat, then cooking on a medium-low heat to create a concentrated heat circulation around the chicken so that the chicken can cook evenly.

Hint: This marinade is a healthier version than store-bought marinades, and makes for an easy addition to meats, fish or vegetables at barbecues.

Per serving: Calories: 139 Protein: 23g Carbs: 4g Fiber: 1g Sugar: 1g Fat: 3g

Baked Parmesan & Herb Coated Chicken Strips

SERVES: 2 / PREP TIME: 10 MINUTES / COOK TIME: 20 MINUTES

This healthy chicken strip recipe uses egg white for dredging, and is baked rather than fried.

1 oz. low fat parmesan cheese, grated
1/4 cup whole wheat breadcrumbs
1 tsp. dried basil
1 tsp. dried oregano
1 tsp. dried thyme
1/2 tsp. paprika
1/4 tsp. sea salt

1 large egg, white only
6 oz. skinless chicken breasts, sliced into 1-inch thick strips

- Preheat the oven to 400°F and line a baking sheet with parchment paper.
- Combine the grated parmesan cheese with the breadcrumbs, dried herbs, paprika, and sea salt. Spread over a shallow dish.
- Whisk the egg white and pour into another shallow dish.
- Dredge the chicken strips in the whisked egg white, and then coat them evenly in the breadcrumbs.
- Arrange the chicken strips onto the baking sheet and bake for 15 to 20 minutes, or until the chicken is cooked through.
- Serve with a crispy lettuce salad.

Hint: Use eggless mayonnaise or olive oil for dredging if opting for a dairy free meal.

Per serving: Calories: 236 Protein: 35g Carbs: 13g Fiber: 2g Sugar: 1g Fat: 5g

Juicy Jerk Chicken

SERVES: 2 / PREP TIME: 5 MINUTES / COOK TIME: 20 MINUTES

This low fat alternative to the Caribbean favorite makes it possible to enjoy without the guilt but with all the flavor!

Olive oil cooking spray
1/8 cup minced onion
1/2 clove garlic, minced
6 oz. skinless chicken breasts, cubed
1 tbsp. Splenda® brown sugar
1/8 cup mango chutney
1 tbsp. Dijon mustard
1 tsp. garam masala
1/2 tsp. salt

- Heat a nonstick frying pan over medium heat.
- Spray with the cooking spray.
- Add the onions and garlic and sauté until the onions are translucent.
- Add the chicken cubes and sear for 5 to 6 minutes, or until the sides are evenly browned.
- While the chicken is cooking, mix together the brown sugar, chutney, mustard, garam masala, and salt in small bowl until well combined.
- Stir the sauce into the pan.
- Reduce the heat, cover the pan with a lid, and allow the chicken to simmer in the sauce for 10 to 12 minutes, or until it is cooked through.

Hint: Delicious when served with a crisp green iceberg lettuce salad.

Per serving: Calories: 236 Protein: 35g Carbs: 13g Fiber: 2g Sugar: 1g Fat: 5g

Chicken Simmered with Black Beans

SERVES: 2 / PREP TIME: 5 MINUTES / COOK TIME: 25 MINUTES

The juices of the chicken blend perfectly with the black beans in this simmering stew.

1/2 tsp. olive oil
6 oz. skinless chicken breasts, cubed
1 tsp. curry powder
1/2 tsp. ground cumin
1/2 tsp. garlic powder
1/2 tsp. paprika
1/4 tsp. red pepper flakes

1/4 tsp. freshly ground black pepper
2 tbsp. low sodium chicken stock
Juice of 1 lime
1/4 cup canned black beans, drained and rinsed

- Heat the olive oil in a nonstick large pan over medium heat and sear the chicken cubes until browned on all sides.
- Add the curry powder, ground cumin, garlic powder, paprika, red pepper flakes, black pepper, chicken stock, and lime juice to the pan.
- Cover the pan with a lid, and cook over medium-low heat for another 10 to 15 minutes, or until the chicken is cooked through.
- Add the black beans to the pan, and simmer covered for 5 minutes until the beans are heated through.

Hint: To serve with a tangy salsa, pulse together 1/4 cup red bell peppers with 1/8 cup red onions. Add 2 tablespoons of lime juice, and top with the desired amount of fresh cilantro, mangoes, and peaches.

Per serving: Calories: 144 Protein: 22g Carbs: 8g Fiber: 3g Sugar: 1g Fat: 5g

One Dish Greek Baked Chicken

SERVES: 2 / PREP TIME: 10 MINUTES / COOK TIME: 45 MINUTES

A lovely herby chicken dish, perfect with an iceberg lettuce and cucumber salad. Dollop with low fat yogurt for a creamier sauce.

Olive oil cooking spray
2 ripe beef tomatoes, finely chopped
1 tbsp. balsamic vinegar
2 small skinless chicken breasts
2 tsp. minced garlic
1 tbsp. dried oregano
1 tsp. chopped chives

1/2 cup reduced sodium chicken stock
1/4 cup reduced sodium green olives stuffed with pimiento, thickly sliced

- Preheat the oven to 400°F.
- Spray an ovenproof dish with cooking spray.
- Marinate the tomatoes with the balsamic vinegar, and set aside.
- Rub the chicken breasts with the minced garlic, dried oregano, and chives.
- Pour the chicken stock into the oven dish and arrange the chicken breasts in the dish.
- Bake for 20 minutes.
- Remove the dish from the oven, and reduce the temperature to 350°F.
- Flip over the chicken breasts, and add the marinated tomatoes and olives to the dish.
- Return to the oven for another 20 to 25 minutes, or until the chicken is cooked through and the tomatoes are softened.

Hint: If the chicken is browning too quickly, cover the dish with a sheet of aluminum foil. To create a thicker sauce, after the dish is cooked, fork-mash the tomatoes and combine well with the juices released from the chicken. Serve with a large iceberg lettuce and cucumber salad, and top with a dollop of low fat yogurt.

Per serving: Calories: 177 Protein: 23g Carbs: 13g Fiber: 1g Sugar: 7g Fat: 4g

Red Wine Chicken

SERVES: 2 / PREP TIME: 5 MINUTES / COOK TIME: 45 MINUTES

Try using a Pinot Noir for this dish, as it has a lower carbohydrate content than a Shiraz or Zinfandel.

6 oz. skinless chicken breasts, cut into 2-inch thick slices	7 oz. canned tomatoes, chopped
Olive oil cooking spray	1/2 cup reduced sodium chicken stock
1/4 cup chopped onions	1/2 cup dry red wine
1/2 clove garlic, minced	1 tsp. dried basil
1 cup mushrooms, sliced	1/2 tsp. dried oregano
1 red bell pepper, seeds removed and sliced	1 large bay leaf
	1/2 tsp. freshly ground black pepper

- Spray the chicken slices with the cooking spray, and sear them in a preheated, deep, nonstick pan.
- Cook for 10-15 minutes, turning once half way through.
- Ensure that the chicken is cooked through, then remove from the pan, and set aside.
- Add the onions and garlic to the pan, and sauté for 5 minutes until the onions are soft and translucent.
- Add the mushrooms and bell pepper and continue cooking for 5 minutes until softened.
- Add the tomatoes, chicken stock, red wine, dried basil, dried oregano, bay leaf, black pepper, and cooked chicken to the pan.
- Bring the sauce to a boil, then reduce the heat and simmer uncovered for 15 to 20 minutes, or until the sauce is reduced by a third.

Per serving: Calories: 222 Protein: 26g Carbs: 19g Fiber: 14g Sugar: 8g Fat: 4g

Sweet and Tangy Chicken with Pumpkin Purée

SERVES: 2 / PREP TIME: 15 MINUTES / COOK TIME: 25 MINUTES

This autumn dish uses canned pumpkin purée, and can be enjoyed all year round.

Zest and juice of 1 lime
1 tbsp. yacon root syrup
2 tbsp. chopped lemongrass, and 1 stalk lemongrass, bruised
2 x small skinless chicken breasts
1 tbsp. ghee
1/2 cup canned pumpkin purée

- To make the marinade:
- Mix together the lime zest, lime juice, yacon root syrup, and chopped lemongrass in a bowl, and set aside.
- Make a few scores on each chicken breast with a sharp knife.
- Rub the marinade onto the chicken breasts, taking care to also rub into the scores. This will help the meat absorb more of the flavor. Set aside to rest for 15 minutes.
- Meantime, preheat the grill/broiler, and line the grill tray with foil.
- Grill the chicken breasts for 10 to 15 minutes, or until they are cooked through. Remove from the grill and set aside for the meat to rest.
- To make the pumpkin purée:
- Heat the ghee in a small frying pan over low heat, and lightly fry the lemongrass stalk until its fragrance is released.
- Stir in the pumpkin purée and allow to cook for a few minutes until the purée is heated through.
- Discard the lemongrass stalk.
- Divide the pumpkin purée between 2 plates and arrange the chicken breasts on the top to serve.

Per serving: Calories: 171 Protein: 20g Carbs: 8g Fiber: 2g Sugar: 2g Fat: 5g

Low-Carb Chicken Tortillas

SERVES: 2 / PREP TIME: 5 MINUTES / COOK TIME: 15 MINUTES

Use a low-carb tortilla and iceberg lettuce to indulge guiltlessly in a much loved classic dish.

Olive oil cooking spray	1/4 tsp. paprika
1/4 red pepper, deseeded and sliced thinly	1/4 tsp. cumin
1/4 yellow pepper, deseeded and sliced thinly	1/4 tsp. dried oregano
6 oz. skinless chicken breasts, cut into thin strips	2 low-carb tortillas
	2 cups iceberg lettuce, finely shredded

- Preheat the oven to 325°F.
- Lightly spray a nonstick frying pan with the cooking spray, and heat over medium heat.
- Add the peppers and sauté until they are softened.
- Add the chicken, paprika, cumin, and dried oregano to the peppers.
- Continue cooking for 15 minutes or until the chicken is cooked through.
- When the chicken is cooking, the tortillas can be wrapped in foil and warmed for 5 minutes.
- To assemble:
- Spoon half of the chicken into the center of each tortilla and top with a cup of shredded lettuce.
- Roll the tortilla and serve warm.

Hint: To serve with a salsa, combine some vine-ripened tomatoes with garlic-infused oil and cilantro in a bowl, and season well with black pepper. This salsa can be made in advance and chilled for greater flavor.

Per serving: Calories: 196 Protein: 26g Carbs: 3g Fiber: 1g Sugar: 2g Fat: 4g

Stuffed Chicken

SERVES: 2 / PREP TIME: 1 HOUR / COOK TIME: 40 MINUTES

This is a juicy, baked chicken dish that can be paired easily with a green bean or fruit salad.

For the Salad:
1/2 cup fresh green beans, trimmed, blanched, and cooled
1/2 cup cherry tomatoes, halved
1/4 red onion, finely chopped
1/2 clove garlic, minced
1 tsp. balsamic vinegar

Freshly ground black pepper, to taste
2x small skinless chicken breasts
2 tbsp. low fat spreadable cheese

- To make the green bean and tomato salad:
- Combine the green beans, cherry tomatoes, onions, garlic, and balsamic vinegar in a bowl.
- Season well with freshly ground black pepper.
- Set aside to chill for an hour.
- Preheat the oven to 400°F and line a baking tray with parchment paper.
- Cut a slit in the chicken breasts to form a pocket.
- Season well with black pepper and stuff 1 tbsp. cheese into each cavity. Secure with a toothpick if needed.
- Bake for 35 to 40 minutes, or until the chicken is cooked through. Serve with the green bean and tomato salad.

Hint: If seasonal fruits are available, combine peaches and apples with apple cider vinegar, top with some fresh mint leaves, and serve as a refreshing side to this stuffed chicken dish.

Per serving: Calories: 140 Protein: 20g Carbs: 7g Fiber: 2g Sugar: 2g Fat: 4g

Cheesy Chicken and Cauliflower Bake

SERVES: 2 / PREP TIME: 5 MINUTES / COOK TIME: 45 MINUTES

This colorful dish packs in the extra nutrients from the colored varieties of cauliflowers. The purple cauliflower is rich in anthocyanins that give the same purple tint to the 'superberries', while the orange cauliflowers are packed with carotenoids beneficial for great skin and eyesight.

Olive oil cooking spray
6 oz. skinless chicken breast(s), cubed
1/3 cup purple cauliflower florets
1/3 cup orange or yellow cauliflower florets
1/3 cup white or green cauliflower florets
1/4 cup low fat parmesan cheese, grated

- Preheat the oven to 350°F.
- Spray a skillet with nonstick cooking spray and heat over medium heat.
- Add the chicken cubes and sear for 15 minutes until the chicken is lightly browned.
- Add the cauliflower florets to the chicken and top with the grated parmesan cheese.
- Place the skillet in the oven and bake for 30 minutes.

Hint: Colored cauliflower can also be pulsed into a rice-like texture and used as a colorful and healthy substitute for fried 'rice' or pizza 'crust'.

Per serving: Calories: 162 Protein: 27g Carbs: 3g Fiber: 1g Sugar: 2g Fat: 5g

Chicken and Lotus Root Soup

SERVES: 1 / PREP TIME: 5 MINUTES / COOK TIME: 6-7 HOURS SLOW COOKER

A light, clear chicken soup for the soul.

---

3 1/2 oz. lotus roots
3 oz. skinless chicken breast
1 cup reduced sodium chicken stock
1 cup water
1/2 carrot, diced

- Combine the ingredients in a slow cooker.
- Set on LOW for 6-7 hours.
- Serve piping hot.

Per serving: Calories: 212 Protein: 26g Carbs: 26g Fiber: 6g Sugar: 1g Fat: 2g

Stuffed Cubanelle Peppers

SERVES: 2 / PREP TIME: 15 MINUTES / COOK TIME: 6-8 HOURS SLOW COOKER

Sweet cubanelle peppers and ground turkey are slow cooked to a sweet blend of flavour.

6 oz. lean ground turkey
1 tsp. dried rosemary
1/2 tsp. garlic infused oil
1 tbsp. onions, chopped
2 beef tomatoes, finely diced
1 tbsp. chives, finely chopped
Freshly ground black pepper

2 large cubanelle peppers

- In a medium bowl, mix together the ground turkey, dried rosemary, garlic-infused oil, chopped onions, diced tomatoes, and chives, and season well with freshly ground black pepper.
- Set aside to marinate for 15 minutes.
- Make an incision across the length of the cubanelle peppers, and remove any seeds and membranes.
- Divide the marinated ground turkey between the peppers.
- Place the peppers in a heatproof dish that will fit the slow cooker snugly.
- Cook on LOW for 6 to 8 hours.
- During cooking, spoon the released juices over the peppers for extra flavor.

Hint: A perfect dish to prepare before heading out for the day. If preferred, it can also be cooked on HIGH for 3 to 4 hours.

Hint: The peppers can be made in bulk and enjoyed later with a helping of cooling low fat natural yogurt.

Per serving: Calories: 191 Protein: 22g Carbs: 18g Fiber: 4g Sugar: 12g Fat: 5g

Airfried Herbed Chicken Breasts with Balsamic Cherry Tomato Salad

SERVES: 2 / PREP TIME: 35 MINUTES / COOK TIME: 30 MINUTES

Airfrying is an excellent way to get crisp and moist results from chicken breasts without the use of oil.

2x small skinless chicken breasts
1/2 tsp. ground ginger
1/2 tsp. cumin
1/2 tsp. coriander seeds, ground
1/2 tsp. dried parsley flakes
1 tsp. freshly ground black pepper
1 cup cherry tomatoes, halved

1 tsp. balsamic vinegar

- Make incisions into the chicken breasts using a sharp knife.
- Rub well with the combined ground ginger, cumin, coriander seeds, dried parsley flakes, and black pepper. Set aside to rest for 30 minutes.
- Preheat the Airfryer to 350ºF.
- Arrange the chicken breasts in the Airfryer Basket and set the time for 30 minutes. Halfway through the cooking time, flip the chicken breasts to allow even cooking.
- While the chicken is cooking, combine the cherry tomatoes and balsamic vinegar, and chill until ready to serve.

Hint: If you don't have an airfryer, use olive oil cooking spray and a hot skillet to sauté the chicken breasts for 7-8 minutes on each side until thoroughly cooked through.

Hint: Halved tomatoes release juices that blend well with the balsamic vinegar, and in return lets the tomatoes absorb more flavor from the combined juices.

Per serving: Calories: 122 Protein: 20g Carbs: 5g Fiber: 2g Sugar: 2g Fat: 4g

SOUPS, STEWS & STOCKS

Weight Loss Fish Stock

SERVES: 8 / PREP TIME: 5 MINUTES / COOK TIME: 1 HOUR

A healthy, homemade stock recipe that can be used as a soup base for a quick fish soup, noodle soup, or risotto.

3 lb fish bones, including heads
3 pt water
1 large carrot, chopped
2 leeks, chopped
2 onions, chopped
1 tbsp. black peppercorns

- Place the fish bones and water in a large stockpot, and bring to a boil.
- Reduce the heat, and simmer for 20 minutes.
- Strain the stock through a muslin cloth and ensure that all the bones are removed.
- Return the stock to the pot, and add in the carrot, leeks, onions, and peppercorns.
- Bring to the boil again, and simmer for 40 minutes.
- Remove the vegetables from the stock, and strain again through the muslin cloth.
- Transfer to containers and allow the stock to cool completely before storing.

Hint: To make a hearty fish soup, add tomatoes and ginger slices to the stock and allow to simmer over a low heat until the tomatoes are softened and the ginger flavor is released. Add fish slices 5 minutes towards the end of the cooking time.

Per 1 cup serving: Calories: 5 Protein: 1g Carbs: 0g Fiber: 0g Sugar: 0g Fat: 0g

Collard Greens Soup Topped with Sage Mushrooms

SERVES: 2 / PREP TIME: 5 MINUTES / COOK TIME: 45 MINUTES

An ideal first course that gets its great flavor from shiitake mushrooms and dried sage.

1 tsp. olive oil	A pinch of freshly ground black pepper, to taste
1 tsp. smoked paprika	2 cups collard greens, loosely packed, big stems removed
1 tsp. cumin	For the sage mushrooms:
2 medium carrots, sliced	Olive oil cooking spray
2 cups water	1/2 cup shiitake mushrooms
½ cup cherry tomatoes	1 tsp. dried sage
3 tbsp. lemon juice	

- Heat the olive oil in a nonstick soup pot over low heat and gently fry the paprika and cumin.
- Increase to medium heat and add the carrots and 1/4 cup water.
- Cover and cook for 10 minutes, stirring occasionally.
- Add in the rest of the ingredients for the soup and increase to medium-high heat to let the soup come to a boil.
- Reduce the heat to medium, and let the soup simmer uncovered for 30-35 minutes, or until the vegetables are tender.
- While the soup is simmering, sauté the shiitake mushrooms.
- To make the shiitake mushrooms:
- Lightly spray a nonstick frying pan with olive oil cooking spray.
- Allow the pan to get very hot before adding the mushrooms as this will prevent the mushrooms from releasing their liquids. When the mushrooms are shrivelled, season with the dried sage.
- Serve the soup with a sprinkling of the sage mushrooms.

Per 1 cup serving: Calories: 101 Protein: 3g Carbs: 16g Fiber: 4g Sugar: 6g Fat: 3g

Carrot and Potato Soup

SERVES: 2 / PREP TIME: 5 MINUTES / COOK TIME: 25 MINUTES

A classic dish, suitable for a vegetarian and weight loss diet.

---

1 cup reduced sodium vegetable stock
1/2 cup scallions (green tips only), sliced
2 medium potatoes, diced
2 large carrots, diced
1 1/2 tbsp. fresh cilantro, chopped, plus more for garnishing

1/4 cup almond milk

- Bring 2 tbsp. stock to the boil in a deep pot.
- Add the scallions and stir gently for 1 to 2 minutes.
- Add the potatoes and carrots to the pot, and cook over low heat for 5 minutes, stirring occasionally.
- Add the remaining stock to the saucepan and turn up the heat to bring the soup to a rolling boil.
- Reduce the heat, cover and allow to simmer for 10 to 15 minutes until the vegetables are softened.
- Remove the soup from the heat, and add in the fresh cilantro.
- Set the soup aside to cool.
- When the soup is cool enough to handle, blend with a handheld blender until the soup reaches your desired consistency.
- Return the soup to a low heat and stir in the almond milk.
- Serve warm topped with fresh cilantro.

Per serving: Calories: 145 Protein: 6g Carbs: 28g Fiber: 4g Sugar: 6g Fat: 2g

Red Pepper and Tomato Soup

SERVES: 4 / PREP TIME: 5 MINUTES / COOK TIME: 35 MINUTES

Another great soup that is filling yet light on calories.

---

2 red peppers, deseeded & cut into strips	3 tbsp. fresh parsley
2 large carrots, peeled & chopped	
1 tbsp. rice bran oil	
Freshly ground black pepper, to taste	
1 cup low fat vegetable stock	
1 cup canned tomatoes, chopped	

- Preheat the oven to 400°F.
- Toss the peppers and carrots with the rice bran oil, and arrange them across an oven tray.
- Season well with freshly ground black pepper.
- Roast the vegetables for 20 to 25 minutes, being sure to give the vegetables a stir halfway through cooking.
- Transfer the vegetables with their juices into a deep soup pot.
- Add the vegetable stock and the canned tomatoes to the pot.
- Blend with a handheld blender.
- Bring the soup to a gentle boil to blend the flavors together, and serve warm topped with fresh parsley.

Hint: To add parsnip chips as a topping, slice 1 medium parsnip into thin slices and toss them with a little avocado oil. Arrange them in a single layer on a lined baking tray and bake at 425°F until they are browned and crisp. Allow to cool completely to let the crisps dry out before serving and storing.

Per serving: Calories: 54 Protein: 6g Carbs: 8g Fiber: 3g Sugar: 5g Fat: 1g

Slow Cooker Chicken Soup with Baby Spinach Leaves

SERVES: 2 / PREP TIME: 10 MINUTES / COOK TIME: 6-7 HOURS SLOW COOKER

A delicious soup that can be effortlessly prepared in advance, and enjoyed throughout the day.

2 cups low fat chicken stock	1/2 tsp. dried rosemary
6 oz. skinless chicken breasts, thickly sliced	2 bay leaves
2 large carrots, peeled and diced	1 tbsp. lemon juice
1/2 cup scallions (green tips only), chopped	Freshly ground black pepper, to taste
1/2 tsp. dried thyme	1 cup baby spinach leaves

- Pour the chicken stock into the slow cooker.
- Arrange the remaining ingredients except the baby spinach leaves into the slow cooker.
- Cook for 6 to 7 hours on LOW.
- To serve, top the soup with the baby spinach leaves.

Per serving: Calories: 172 Protein: 23g Carbs: 9g Fiber: 4g Sugar: 4g Fat: 5g

Thai Chicken Soup

SERVES: 2 / PREP TIME: 5 MINUTES / COOK TIME: 30 MINUTES

This clear Thai chicken soup is super easy to put together.

---

1 cup low fat chicken stock
1 cup water
6 oz. skinless chicken breasts, sliced
Freshly ground black pepper, to taste
1/2 tsp. turmeric
1/2 tbsp. galangal, sliced
1 clove garlic, crushed

1 tbsp. sliced scallions - green ends only
1 large tomato, diced
1/3 cup baby corn
1/3 cup snow peas
Juice of 1 lime

- Combine the chicken stock and water in a soup pot, and bring to a boil over high heat.
- Reduce the heat, and add all the remaining ingredients, except for the snow peas and lime juice.
- Bring to a boil again, then reduce the heat so that the soup is simmering for about 20 to 25 minutes.
- Add the snow peas in the last 10 minutes of the cooking time.
- The soup is ready when the chicken is cooked through.
- Stir in the lime juice, and serve warm.

Per serving: Calories: 166 Protein: 23g Carbs: 13g Fiber: 3g Sugar: 4g Fat: 4g

Cherry Tomato Soup

SERVES: 4 / PREP TIME: 5 MINUTES / COOK TIME: 30 MINUTES

This nutritious soup is made with the juices from cherry tomatoes - a definite crowd pleaser!

Olive oil cooking spray
1 large onion, chopped
1 1/2 lb sun sugar tomatoes
1 1/2 lb cherry tomatoes
1 bay leaf
1 tsp. dried thyme
Freshly ground black pepper, as desired

- Lightly spray a large soup pot and heat it over medium heat.
- Add the onions and sauté until the onions have released their flavor and are translucent.
- Add the tomatoes and herbs to the pot.
- Cover the pot with a lid, and simmer the tomatoes on low heat for 20 minutes.
- Allow to rest for 10 minutes.
- Remove the bay leaf from the pot, and blend the soup with a handheld mixer.
- Strain the soup, and season with black pepper to serve.

Hint. This can be made in larger batches in a slow cooker, and is suitable for freezing.

Per serving: Calories: 116 Protein: 6g Carbs: 19g Fiber: 7g Sugar: 12g Fat: 0g

Curried Zucchini Soup

SERVES: 2 / PREP TIME: 5 MINUTES / COOK TIME: 40 MINUTES

A pinch of curry powder gives a kick of taste to this zucchini soup.

Olive oil cooking spray
1 white onion, chopped
2 zucchinis, chopped
1/2 tsp. curry powder
2 cups reduced sodium vegetable stock

- Lightly spray a nonstick pot with the olive oil cooking spray and heat over medium heat.
- Add the onion, zucchinis, and curry powder to the pan, and sauté for 5 to 8 minutes until the onions are translucent and the zucchinis are soft.
- Add the vegetable stock, cover the pot with a fitting lid, and simmer for 30 minutes.
- Blend with a handheld blender, and serve warm.

Hint: To give a smoky, roasted flavor to the soup, roast the vegetables in the oven first, rather than cooking them in the pan.

Per serving: Calories: 77 Protein: 3g Carbs: 14g Fiber: 4g Sugar: 6g Fat: 1g

Rutabaga and Sweet Potato Soup

SERVES: 2 / PREP TIME: 5 MINUTES / COOK TIME: 40 MINUTES

A hearty and filling soup sweetened by the sweet potatoes.

Olive oil cooking spray
1/2 onion, peeled and chopped
1/2 lb rutabaga, peeled and chopped
1/4 lb sweet potatoes, peeled and chopped
2 cups reduced sodium chicken stock

- Preheat the oven to 350°F.
- Lightly spray a baking dish with the olive oil cooking spray, and arrange the onions, rutabaga, and sweet potatoes in the dish.
- Bake for 20 to 25 minutes until the roots are slightly tender.
- Now bring the chicken stock to a slow simmer in a soup pot over medium-high heat.
- Add the root vegetables to the stock and bring to a boil.
- Reduce the heat, and simmer for 15 minutes, or until the roots are completely softened.
- Remove from the heat and allow the soup to cool. When cool enough to handle, blend with a handheld blender, and serve warm.

Hint: Use vegetable stock to make a vegetarian version of the soup.

Per serving: Calories: 147 Protein: 8g Carbs: 31g Fiber: 6g Sugar: 11g Fat: 0g

Slow Cooker Chicken Curry

SERVES: 2 / PREP TIME: 5 MINUTES / COOK TIME: 6-8 HOURS SLOW COOKER

A slow cooked dish that fills the kitchen with the aroma of spices.

Coconut oil cooking spray	1 tsp. cumin
6 oz. skinless chicken breast, cubed	1/2 tsp. paprika
1/4 medium onion, chopped	3/4 tsp. ground cinnamon
1/2 clove garlic, minced	3/4 tsp. ground black pepper
1/2 tsp. fresh ginger, minced	1 bay leaf
1/4 cup reduced sodium tomato paste	1 tsp. cayenne pepper, as desired
1/4 cup low fat Greek yogurt	1/2 cup freshly chopped cilantro, for garnishing
1/2 tbsp. garam masala	

- Lightly spray the base of the slow cooker with the cooking spray.
- Add all the ingredients to the pot (reserve the cilantro for garnishing).
- Mix well, and set to LOW for 6-8 hours.
- Serve with freshly chopped cilantro.

Per serving: Calories: 197 Protein: 23g Carbs: 24g Fiber: 8g Sugar: 5g Fat: 5g

Slow Cooker Chicken Chili

SERVES: 2 / PREP TIME: 5 MINUTES / COOK TIME: 4-5 HOURS SLOW COOKER

So easy to prepare, and the slow cooking releases all the tasty flavors, making this a winner.

1/2 chopped onion
1/2 clove garlic, minced
1 cup bell peppers
1 cup reduced sodium chicken broth
1/2 tsp. cumin
4 oz. ground chicken
1/4 cup canned black beans, drained and rinsed

- Place all the ingredients except the black beans into the slow cooker pot.
- Set the slow cooker to LOW for 4-5 hours.
- An hour before the chili is done, add the black beans to the slow cooker and mix well so that the flavors are well blended.

Hint: Replace the black beans with fava beans to reduce calories and carbohydrate. This recipe is suitable to make a larger batch for freezing.

Per serving: Calories: 113 Protein: 16g Carbs: 10g Fiber: 4g Sugar: 5g Fat: 4g

Roast Turkey Breasts with Brussels Sprouts

SERVES: 2 / PREP TIME: 5 MINUTES / COOK TIME: 40 MINUTES

A festive meal that can be made with very little effort.

2x small skinless turkey breasts
Freshly ground black pepper, to taste
½ tsp. dried oregano
½ tsp. dried thyme
½ tsp. dried sage
1/2 cup reduced sodium chicken stock
1 cup water

1 carrot, peeled and chopped
5 oz brussels sprouts

- Preheat the oven to 450°F.
- Rub the turkey breasts with the combined black pepper, dried oregano, dried thyme, and dried sage.
- Pour the chicken stock and water into an ovenproof dish, and arrange the turkey in the dish.
- Add the carrots to the dish, and bake for 30 to 40 minutes, or until the turkey is cooked through.
- Meanwhile, blanch the brussels sprouts in boiling water for 5 minutes.
- Serve the turkey with the carrots and brussels sprouts, and drizzle over with the released juices from the dish.

Per serving: Calories: 107 Protein: 16g Carbs: 10g Fiber: 4g Sugar: 2g Fat: 5g

Slow Cooker Chicken and Lemon Rice Stew

SERVES: 2 / PREP TIME: 10 MINUTES / COOK TIME: 6-7 HOURS SLOW COOKER

A hearty dinner that can be prepared in the slow-cooker while you are out and about.

Olive oil cooking spray
2x small, skinless chicken breasts, cubed
1 cup reduced sodium chicken stock
1 cup water
1 tsp. dried oregano
A pinch of black pepper

1/2 cup uncooked brown rice, rinsed
1 lemon, juice and grated zest
1 cucumber, washed and sliced

- Lightly spray a nonstick frying pan with olive oil cooking spray.
- Add the chicken cubes and sear until they are browned.
- Transfer the chicken to the slow cooker pot.
- Add the chicken stock, water, dried oregano, black pepper, uncooked brown rice, lemon juice, and lemon zest to the pot.
- Mix well, and set the cooker to LOW for 6-7 hours.
- Serve with fresh cucumbers.

Per serving: Calories: 194 Protein: 21g Carbs: 25g Fiber: 2g Sugar: 2g Fat: 4g

Fennel and Ginger Chicken with Asparagus Tips

SERVES: 2 / PREP TIME: 5 MINUTES / COOK TIME: 3 HOURS SLOW COOKER

The bold flavors of fennel, ginger, and garlic are delicious and sure to impress.

2x small skinless, chicken breasts, diced
1/4 tsp. ground black pepper
1 bulb fennel, cored and cut into thin wedges
1 red bell pepper, de-seeded and diced
1 tsp. dried rosemary
1 tsp. ground ginger

1/2 cup recuced sodium chicken stock
1/2 cup water
1 tbsp. dried oregano
7 oz. asparagus tips (not stalks)

- Season the chicken pieces with ground pepper and place them in the slow cooker pot.
- Add the remaining ingredients to the pot.
- Cover and cook on High for 2 1/2 to 3 hours.

Hint: Use spears of asparagus, not their stalks for weight loss cooking.

Per serving: Calories: 121 Protein: 19g Carbs: 7g Fiber: 3g Sugar: 4g Fat: 5g

Carrot and Turkey Soup

SERVES: 2 / PREP TIME: 5 MINUTES / COOK TIME: 30 MINUTES

A simmered soup for a rich flavor.

---

2 cups reduced sodium chicken stock
6 oz. turkey breast, cubed
1 carrot, diced
1 cob of corn, cut into 2-inch thick pieces
1 tbsp. fresh parsley, roughly chopped

- Bring the chicken stock to a boil in a soup pot over high heat.
- Reduce the heat, and add the turkey, carrots, and corn pieces to the pot.
- Ensure that the ingredients are submerged in the stock, and add some water to the pot if necessary.
- Bring to a boil again, then reduce the heat, and simmer for 15 to 20 minutes until the turkey is cooked through.
- Remove the turkey from the soup and set aside to cool.
- When the turkey is cool enough to handle, shred the meat and return to pot, with all its released juices.
- Stir through.
- Serve the soup warm, topped with the fresh parsley.

Hint: The soup should have a rich flavor, but if it is a little watery, continue simmering the soup uncovered after removing the turkey breasts. This will reduce the liquid and enrich the flavor of the soup.

Per serving: Calories: 177 Protein: 23g Carbs: 15g Fiber: 1g Sugar: 2g Fat: 4g

Turkey Goulash with Baby Spinach Leaves

SERVES: 2 / PREP TIME: 5 MINUTES / COOK TIME: 30 MINUTES

The crisp spinach leaves add a crunchy texture to a delicious goulash.

Olive oil cooking spray
6 oz. skinless turkey breast, cubed
1 carrot, diced
1/2 cup green pepper, chopped
4 beef tomatoes, chopped
1 tsp. paprika
Freshly ground black pepper

1 tbsp. reduced sodium tomato paste
1 cup reduced sodium chicken stock
1 cup organic baby spinach leaves
1 tbsp. chives, snipped

- Lightly spray a nonstick frying pan with the olive oil cooking spray and heat on medium heat.
- Add the turkey pieces and sear until they are evenly browned.
- Add the carrot, pepper, tomatoes, paprika, and freshly ground black pepper.
- Cook for 2 minutes and add the tomato paste and stock to the pan.
- Bring to a boil, and then reduce the heat.
- Cover the goulash with a lid, and simmer for 20 minutes until the sauce is thick and the flavors are well blended. Stir occasionally to prevent the sauce from sticking to the pan.
- Serve hot topped with the baby spinach leaves and freshly snipped chives.

Hint: Replace the spinach leaves with baby arugula leaves for a sharper taste to the goulash.

Per serving: Calories: 210 Protein: 30g Carbs: 20g Fiber: 3g Sugar: 12g Fat: 4g

Cabbage Soup with Arugula Leaves

SERVES: 2 / PREP TIME: 5 MINUTES / COOK TIME: 45 MINUTES

Arugula leaves are popular to use in miso-based noodle soups. Mixed with cannellini beans, this is a low calorie, low fat, and high fiber soup.

Olive oil cooking spray
1/4 large onion, diced
1/2 clove garlic, minced
1 cup reduced sodium chicken stock
1 head of cabbage, chopped
1 cup cherry tomatoes
7 fl oz. canned cannellini beans
2 cups arugula leaves

- Lightly spray a large soup pot with cooking spray and heat over medium heat.
- Add the onions and garlic to the pot, and sauté until their fragrances are released.
- Add the chicken stock, cabbage, and tomatoes to the pot. Add more water if necessary to just about cover the cabbage.
- Bring to a boil, then reduce the heat, and simmer until the cabbage is tender, about 30 minutes.
- Add the cannellini beans, and simmer for another 10 minutes.
- Serve topped with the fresh arugula leaves.

Hint: For a stronger cabbage flavor, roast the chopped cabbage with fennel seeds before cooking in the stock.

Per serving: Calories: 128 Protein: 8g Carbs: 17g Fiber: 10g Sugar: 6g Fat: 0g

Cumin and Turmeric Fish Stew

SERVES: 2 / PREP TIME: 5 MINUTES / COOK TIME: 25 MINUTES

A light dish cooked with cumin and turmeric spices, lending the fish soup a deep flavor.

Olive oil cooking spray
1 tsp. grated fresh ginger
1 tsp. ground cumin
1 tsp. turmeric
1 tsp. cayenne pepper
1 cup cherry tomatoes
9 oz. water

6 oz. firm white fish fillets (cod, snapper or ling), cut into chunks
Freshly ground black pepper
1 tbsp. fresh cilantro leaves

- Lightly spray a large heavy based pot with the cooking spray, and heat over medium heat.
- Gently fry the ginger, cumin, and turmeric for about 2 minutes until the flavors are released.
- Add the cayenne pepper, tomatoes, and water to the pot, and bring to a boil.
- Reduce the heat, and simmer for 10 to 15 minutes.
- Add the fish chunks to the soup and simmer for 5 minutes, or until the fish is almost cooked through and tender.
- Season to taste with freshly ground black pepper, and garnish with the fresh cilantro leaves.

Hint: Use homemade fish stock to replace the water for a richer taste.

Per serving: Calories: 128 Protein: 16 g Carbs: 10g Fiber: 5g Sugar: 5g Fat: 4g

Super Greens Soup

SERVES: 2 / PREP TIME: 5 MINUTES / COOK TIME: 25 MINUTES

A tasty soup made with a beef stock base.

Olive oil cooking spray
1/2 white onion, finely diced
1 garlic clove, minced
2 cups reduced sodium beef stock
4 cups baby spinach leaves
4 cups watercress
2 cups frozen garden peas, defrosted

1 cup water
1 tbsp. fresh parsley, chopped

- Spray the cooking spray in a soup pot, and heat over medium heat.
- Add the onions and garlic and sauté for 5 minutes until soft.
- Add the stock and water and bring to a rolling boil.
- Add the spinach leaves and watercress and turn down to a simmer for 20 minutes.
- Add the peas in the last 5 minutes.
- Remove from the heat and allow the soup to cool slightly before blending with a handheld blender.
- Serve warm, topped with the chopped fresh parsley.

Hint: Make this vegetarian and vegan friendly by simply using vegetable stock instead of beef stock.

Per serving: Calories: 116 Protein: 10 g Carbs: 14g Fiber: 5g Sugar: 6g Fat: 1g

High Protein Chickpea and Garden Pea Stew

SERVES: 8 / PREP TIME: 5 MINUTES / COOK TIME: 25 MINUTES

This recipe uses paprika to add a nice spice to the stew.

1/2 cup reduced sodium chicken stock
2 tsp. paprika
Freshly ground black pepper, to taste
1 cup canned chickpeas, drained and rinsed
1 cup frozen green peas, defrosted
1 tbsp. fresh cilantro, chopped

1/2 tbsp. lemon juice

- Combine the chicken stock, paprika, and black pepper in a soup pot and bring to a boil.
- Reduce the heat and add the chickpeas.
- Simmer covered for 15 minutes, or until the chickpeas are softened.
- Add the green peas and cilantro, and heat through for 5 minutes.
- Serve hot, and drizzle over the lemon juice.

Per serving: Calories: 168 Protein: 11g Carbs: 31g Fiber: 11g Sugar: 4g Fat: 2g

SAUCES & CONDIMENTS

Creamy Basil Pesto

SERVES: 8 / PREP TIME: 5 MINUTES / COOK TIME: NA

This recipe uses avocado instead of olive oil to give the pesto its creamy consistency.

1 cup fresh basil leaves 1 tbsp. olive oil 1 small ripened avocado 1/4 cup low fat hard cheese 1 tsp. pine nuts 1 tsp. pepper 1 clove garlic, minced	Juice of a lemon

- Combine the ingredients in a food processor, and blend until smooth.

Hint: Add a hint of low fat yogurt to use this pesto as a pasta sauce.

Hint: Skip the nuts if you're not allowed them in your recovery stage - check with your doctor.

Per serving: Calories: 46 Protein: 2g Carbs: 2.5g Fiber: 1g Sugar: 0g Fat: 3.5g

Cannellini Hummus

SERVES: 1 1/2 CUPS / PREP TIME: 5 MINUTES / COOK TIME: NA

A delicious take on the regular chickpea hummus, and so good you can eat it on its own.

15 oz. canned cannellini beans, drained and juice reserved
2 cloves garlic, minced
Juice of 1 lemon
1/3 low fat Greek yogurt
1 tsp. cayenne pepper

- Combine the cannellini beans, garlic, lemon juice, and Greek yogurt in a food processor, and blend until it reaches your desired consistency.
- Top with cayenne pepper before serving.

Hint: Use the pulse button to create a chunkier hummus.

Per 1 1/2 cups): Calories: 344   Protein: 26g Carbs: 72g Fiber: 25g Sugar: 5g Fat: 0g

Baba Ganoush Dip

SERVES: 4 / PREP TIME: 5 MINUTES / COOK TIME: 45 MINUTES

A classic must-make recipe that is sure to please the palate.

---

1 medium eggplant (about 1 lb), halved
1 tsp. olive oil
2 tbsp. light roasted tahini
1/2 tsp. cumin
Juice of 1/2 lemon
1/2 tsp. cayenne pepper
1 clove garlic, minced

1 tbsp. fresh parsley, chopped

- Prick the eggplant in several places with a fork and lay on an oven tray.
- Broil the eggplants on the top oven rack under medium-low heat for 45 minutes, turning every 10 minutes or so, until eggplant is charred all over.
- Remove from the oven and cover very loosely with foil to a low to sweat.
- When cool, remove the skin and transfer the pulp to a blender or food processor.
- Add all remaining ingredients except the fresh parsley and blend until very smooth.
- Transfer to serving bowl and sprinkle with the parsley.

Per serving: Calories: 87 Protein: 1g Carbs: 8g Fiber: 4g Sugar: 3g Fat: 5g

Homemade BBQ Sauce

SERVES: 1 1/2 CUPS / PREP TIME: 5 MINUTES / COOK TIME: 5 MINUTES

A healthy BBQ sauce to accompany summer's grilled dishes.

---

1 1/2 cup reduced sodium tomato paste
1/4 cup apple cider vinegar
1 tbsp. finely chopped onions
1 tsp. minced garlic
Freshly ground black pepper
A dash of TABASCO® hot sauce
1 tbsp. stevia

- Combine the tomato paste and apple cider vinegar in a bowl.
- Heat a small saucepan over low heat, and gradually add the tomato paste mixture a tablespoon at a time to simmer until the sauce starts to thicken.
- Add the onions, garlic, pepper and TABASCO® sauce to the pot, and simmer for 2 minutes.
- Stir in the stevia and remove from the heat.

Hint: The flavor of the sauce is improved from resting, and can be adjusted by adding vinegar or tomato paste. It is an ideal sauce to make the night before.

Per 1 1/2 cups: Calories: 37 Protein: 1g Carbs: 9g Fiber: 2g Sugar: 3g Fat: 0g

Mixed Bean Salsa

SERVES: 2 / PREP TIME: 35 MINUTES / COOK TIME: NA

A low calorie yet filling salsa; suitable as a side to grilled chicken, fish or vegetable chilli dishes.

3 tbsp. canned mixed beans
1 beef tomato, finely diced
1/4 red onion, finely diced
1/2 tbsp. olive oil
1 tsp. red wine vinegar
Juice of 1/2 lemon
Freshly ground black pepper

- Combine all the ingredients in a serving bowl, and chill for at least 30 minutes before serving.

Hint: Reserve the water from the beans to add flavor and replace olive oil in a hummus recipe.

Per serving: Calories: 82 Protein: 3g Carbs: 8g Fiber: 2g Sugar: 3g Fat: 4g

Spicy Lentils

SERVES: 2 / PREP TIME: 5 MINUTES / COOK TIME: 1 HOUR

A great low-calorie side dish that is perfect to pack along for picnics.

1/2 cup lentils
1/2 cup water
1/4 cup onion, chopped
1 tsp. cumin
1 tsp. curry powder

- Combine all the ingredients in a nonstick pot and bring to a boil.
- Reduce the heat to a simmer and leave to cook, covered, for an hour until the lentils are softened.

Per serving: Calories: 52 Protein: 3g Carbs: 9g Fiber: 1g Sugar: 1g Fat: 0g

Parsley Hummus

SERVES: 2 / PREP TIME: 5 MINUTES / COOK TIME: NA

A bright splash of green parsley to the humble hummus will surely excite the palate and adds a fresh herby taste to the traditional dip.

1/4 cup reduced sodium canned chickpeas, juice reserved
Juice of a lemon
Freshly ground black pepper
1 clove garlic, crushed
1/4 cup fresh parsley, chopped
2 tbsp. low fat Greek yogurt

- Combine all the ingredients in a food processor and blend until it reaches your desired consistency (use the reserved juice from the chickpeas like you would use olive oil to adjust the consistency of the hummus.)

Hint: Use chives or cilantro in place of parsley, or toast some sage leaves and crumble over a regular hummus.

Per serving: Calories: 58 Protein: 3g Carbs: 10g Fiber: 2g Sugar: 3g Fat: 1g

Spicy Mango Chutney

SERVES: 2 / PREP TIME: 5 MINUTES / COOK TIME: 15 MINUTES

An indispensable pantry condiment now made healthier.

1/2 tsp. olive oil
1/4 cup onion, finely diced
1 tsp. root ginger, minced
1/4 cup mango, finely diced
1 tsp. mustard seeds
1 tsp. chia seeds

- Heat the olive oil in a nonstick frying pan and sauté the onions until they soften and become translucent, about 5 minutes.
- Add the ginger and stir-fry for another 2 minutes.
- Add the diced mangoes, mustard seeds, and chia seeds to the pan.
- Cover and simmer for 10 to 15 minutes until the flavors and fragrances are released.
- Remove from the heat and allow the chutney to cool completely in the pan before transferring to an airtight container.

Hint: For best flavor, make the chutney the night before serving so that the flavors can blend.

Per serving: Calories: 73 Protein: 2g Carbs: 7g Fiber: 3g Sugar: 3g Fat: 5g

Peach and Mango Salsa

SERVES: 2 / PREP TIME: 5 MINUTES / COOK TIME: NA

A wonderful condiment for the picnic basket.

1/4 cup red onion, finely diced
Juice of a lime
1/2 tsp. apple cider vinegar
1 tsp. freshly ground black pepper
1/4 cup diced mango
1/4 cup chopped peaches
1 tbsp. fresh cilantro, coarsely chopped

- Combine all the ingredients in a bowl and chill for at least 30 minutes.

Per serving: Calories: 36 Protein: 1g Carbs: 10g Fiber: 1g Sugar: 6g Fat: 0g

White Cheese Sauce

SERVES: 5 / PREP TIME: 5 MINUTES / COOK TIME: 10 MINUTES

A healthy recipe to replace a regular béchamel sauce - great with lasagna, pasta, and fish.

1 tbsp. low fat butter
1/4 cup low carb all purpose flour
3/4 cup skim milk
4 oz. low fat soft cheese
1/4 tsp. white pepper

- Melt the butter over low heat in a nonstick frying pan.
- Add the flour to the butter, stirring consistently to get a paste.
- Slowly add in the skim milk and cream cheese, and stir continuously until the sauce thickens.
- Season with the white pepper, and use with desired recipe.

Per serving: Calories: 85 Protein: 7g Carbs: 6g Fiber: 1g Sugar: 4g Fat: 4g

SNACKS & SALADS

Thai 'Rice Noodle' Salad

SERVES: 2 / PREP TIME: 15 MINUTES / COOK TIME: 10 MINUTES

Zucchini noodles are fun to make, and taste delicious and crunchy.

For the salad dressing:	2 zucchinis
2 tbsp. fish sauce	1/2 cup carrot, peeled and grated
1 tbsp. white vinegar	1/4 cup peeled, diced, seeded cucumber
2 tbsp. fresh lime juice	1/4 cup scallions, sliced
	1 tbsp. fresh cilantro leaves, finely chopped
	1 tbsp. fresh mint leaves, finely chopped

- Whisk dressing ingredients in a small bowl and set aside until ready to serve.
- Use a julienne peeler to make zucchini noodles with the zucchinis.
- Mix the zucchini noodles with the salad dressing, and top with the grated carrot, sliced scallions, diced cucumber, fresh cilantro, and fresh mint leaves.

Hint: Use a mix of green and yellow zucchinis to add more color and flavor to the dish. Stop peeling when you reach the seeds of the zucchinis as they will not hold their shape.

Per serving: Calories: 79 Protein: 4g Carbs: 13g Fiber: 3g Sugar: 8g Fat: 0g

Cucumber and Sundried Tomatoes

SERVES: 2 / PREP TIME: 5 MINUTES / COOK TIME: NA

A refreshing salad with a meaty flavorsome texture from the tomatoes.

---

4 oz. sundried tomatoes, finely chopped
1 cup cucumbers, peeled and chopped
1 tsp. olive oil
Juice of a lime
Freshly ground black pepper

- Combine the sundried tomatoes, cucumbers, olive oil, and lime juice in a serving bowl.
- Serve immediately.

Hint: Alternatively, broil your own halved tomatoes under a medium heat. Just drizzle 1 tsp. olive oil and shake on dried herbs of your choice, along with a little salt and pepper. Once soft and bubbling (about 10 minutes), remove and layer over the cucumbers.

Per serving: Calories: 134 Protein: 2g Carbs: 9g Fiber: 2g Sugar: 1g Fat: 3g

Spiced Lentils on a Baby Spinach Bed

SERVES: 2 / PREP TIME: 5 MINUTES / COOK TIME: 30 MINUTES

The taste of the spiced lentils are balanced with the fresh baby spinach leaves in this dish.

1 cup canned red lentils, drained
1 bay leaf
1 tsp. cumin
1 tsp. turmeric
1 cup baby spinach leaves, washed

- In a soup pot, submerge the lentils in 2 1/4 cups water.
- Add a bay leaf to the pot, and bring to a boil.
- Lower the heat and cook for 20 to 30 minutes, or until the lentils are softened.
- Drain the lentils and transfer to a bowl.
- Season the lentils with the cumin and turmeric.
- Arrange the baby spinach leaves on a serving plate and top over with the cooked lentils.

Hint: If using dried lentils, soak in warm water overnight before using.

Per serving: Calories: 126 Protein: 8g Carbs: 22g Fiber: 5g Sugar: 1g Fat: 1g

Edamame and Avocado Dip

SERVES: 4 / PREP TIME: 5 MINUTES / COOK TIME: NA

A must try creamy and nutty dip that can be hand mashed in minutes!

---

1 small avocado
12 oz. cooked edamame beans
1/2 onion, chopped
1/2 cup low fat Greek yogurt
Juice of a lemon

- Mash the avocado and edamame beans with a fork until smooth.
- Stir in the onions, Greek yogurt, and lemon juice.
- Serve immediately.

Hint: If using frozen edamame beans, steam the beans rather than boil them, to retain more flavor and nutrients. This dip can also be spiced up with a dash of siracha sauce.

Per serving: Calories: 120 Protein: 9g Carbs: 11g Fiber: 4g Sugar: 4g Fat: 5g

White Wine Chicken and Spinach Salad

SERVES: 2 / PREP TIME: 5 MINUTES / COOK TIME: 20 MINUTES

A traditional pairing of white wine and chicken, without all the heavy cream that usually comes with it. Light and refreshing.

- 1 oz. dry, white wine
- 2 tbsp. ginger
- 1 scallion stem, finely chopped
- 6 oz. skinless, chicken breasts
- 1 cup baby spinach leaves, washed

- To make the marinade:
- Combine the wine, ginger, and scallions in a small bowl.
- Make incisions in the chicken breasts and rub well with the marinade.
- Place the chicken breasts in a heatproof dish, and steam for 15 to 20 minutes, or until the chicken is cooked through.
- To serve:
- Arrange the baby spinach leaves on two serving plates. Slice the chicken breasts and arrange the slices on the spinach beds. Drizzle the released juices from the dish over the chicken and enjoy.

Hint: To make a sauce:
Pour the released juices from the dish into a small saucepan, and some chicken stock. Season well with pepper, simmer to reduce the stock into a thickened sauce.

Per serving: Calories: 135 Protein: 18 Carbs: 2g Fiber: 1g Sugar: 0g Fat: 5g

Ginger Quinoa with Balsamic-Roasted Brussels

SERVES: 2 / PREP TIME: 5 MINUTES / COOK TIME: 25 MINUTES

This dish explodes with flavor and is a low calorie and low carb, yet filling meal.

---

1 cup brussels sprouts, halved
1 tsp. balsamic vinegar
Freshly ground black pepper
2 oz. quinoa
4 oz. water
1 tsp. finely grated ginger
1 tsp. ground cumin
1 tsp. ground coriander seeds
1/2 tsp. salt

- Preheat the oven to 35°F.
- To make the balsamic-roasted brussels sprouts:
- Combine the brussels sprouts with the balsamic vinegar, and season well with freshly ground black pepper.
- Bake in the oven for 20 to 25 minutes, or until the brussels sprouts are softened.
- Meanwhile, rinse the quinoa well in cold water and drain.
- Boil the quinoa with the water, ginger, cumin, ground coriander, and salt for 10 to 15 minutes, or until nearly all the water has been absorbed.
- Serve hot, topped with the roasted brussels sprouts, and spoon over with the juices from the baking dish.

Hint: Quinoa can also be cooked in a rice cooker, using the quinoa to water ratio 1:2.

Per serving: Calories: 134 Protein: 5g Carbs: 24g Fiber: 4g Sugar: 2g Fat: 2g

Cucumber Bites Stuffed with Lemon-Dill Cottage Cheese

SERVES: 2 / PREP TIME: 10 MINUTES / COOK TIME: NA

A fun to prepare snack, high in protein and refreshing to enjoy.

---

1 small cucumber, cut into 1-inch thick slices
3/4 cup low fat cottage cheese
1 tsp. fresh dill, chopped
1 tsp. fresh parsley, chopped
1 scallion stem, sliced
Juice of 1/2 lemon

Freshly ground black pepper

- For each cucumber slice, use a cookie cutter to core the center so it resembles a doughnut ring.
- Combine the cottage cheese, dill, parsley, scallions, and lemon juice in a bowl, and season well with freshly ground black pepper.
- Stuff each cucumber with the cottage cheese filling, and chill until ready to serve.

Hint: It is also fancy to serve the cottage cheese filling as a dip, accompanied by vegetable sticks.

Per serving: Calories: 77 Protein: 9g Carbs: 6g Fiber: 0g Sugar: 5g Fat: 2g

Nutella® Protein Bars

SERVES: 8 BARS / PREP TIME: 10 MINUTES / COOK TIME: 20 MINUTES

Yes, Nutella. Here is a specially-crafted recipe to incorporate Nutella® into your weight-loss diet.

1 cup wholegrain rolled oats
1/4 cup chocolate protein powder
1/2 tbsp. ground flax
1/2 tbsp. oat bran
1/2 tsp. ground cinnamon
1/4 tsp. sea salt
1 tbsp. Nutella®

1/8 cup coconut oil
1/8 cup honey
1/4 cup chocolate skim milk

- Preheat the oven to 350°F, and lightly spray a 4x5-inch baking tray with cooking spray.
- Combine the wholegrain rolled oats, chocolate protein powder, ground flax, oat bran, ground cinnamon, and salt in a large bowl. Set aside.
- Whisk together the Nutella®, coconut oil, honey, and chocolate skim milk in a medium bowl until well combined.
- Add the wet ingredients to the dry ingredients and stir until well combined.
- Pour the mixture into the prepared baking pan, and use a spatula to spread the mixture evenly in the pan. Press down firmly.
- Bake for 15 to 20 minutes, or until the edges begin to turn golden brown.
- Remove the pan from the oven, and allow to cool for 20 minutes before slicing into 8 equal pieces.

Per serving (1 bar): Calories: 114 Protein: 7g Carbs: 15g Fiber: 2g Sugar: 7g Fat: 5g

Zucchini Bread

SERVES: 8 / PREP TIME: 10 MINUTES / COOK TIME: 1 HOUR

The roasted walnut spray adds a nutty flavor to the bread, without the calories.

Roasted walnut oil spray
1 1/2 cups whole wheat flour
1/2 tsp. baking soda
1/2 tsp. baking powder
1/2 tsp. salt
1/2 tsp. ground cinnamon
1/4 tsp. ground nutmeg

1 1/2 cups shredded zucchini (squeezed and drained in a paper towel)
1/2 cup stevia
3 tbsp. unsweetened applesauce
1/2 cup plain low fat Greek yogurt
1 large egg
1 tsp. vanilla extract

- Preheat the oven to 350°F, and lightly coat a 9x5-inch baking pan with the roasted walnut oil spray.
- Whisk together the whole wheat flour, baking soda, baking powder, salt, ground cinnamon, and ground nutmeg in a large bowl. Set aside.
- In another bowl, combine shredded zucchini, stevia, unsweetened applesauce, low fat yogurt, egg, and vanilla extract.
- Add the wet ingredients to the dry ingredients and mix until well combined.
- Pour the batter into the prepared pan, and bake for 50 to 60 minutes, or until a toothpick inserted into the center comes out clean.
- Remove from the oven, and let the zucchini bread cool in the pan for 10 minutes before transferring onto a wire rack.
- Allow the bread to cool completely before slicing to let it reabsorb the juices released during cooking.

Hint: Replace the roasted walnut spray with vegetable oil spray for a nut-free recipe.

Per serving: Calories: 162 Protein: 6g Carbs: 33g Fiber: 6g Sugar: 2g Fat: 2g

Rice Cooker Quinoa

SERVES: 2 / PREP TIME: 5 MINUTES / COOK TIME: 20 MINUTES

This quinoa is cooked in a water broth infused with ginger, spring onions, and lemon zest, and is full of flavor and fragrance when cooked.

2 oz. quinoa
4 oz. water
2 bunches green onions, chopped
2 tsp. shredded ginger
1 tsp. freshly ground black pepper
1 tsp. ginger infused olive oil
1 tbsp. shredded lemon zest

- Wash the quinoa thoroughly and drain. This will remove the bitterness.
- Combine the quinoa, the water, and all the remaining ingredients in a rice-cooker pot, and set to COOK.

Per serving: Calories: 134 Protein: 5g Carbs: 21g Fiber: 3g Sugar: 0g Fat: 4g

Parsley Sautéed Mushrooms

SERVES: 2 / PREP TIME: 5 MINUTES / COOK TIME: 10 MINUTES

This is the perfect pairing of mushrooms and parsley, and is great with chicken, topped over soup, or combined with other roasted vegetables.

Olive oil cooking spray
4 cups button mushrooms, sliced
1 cup fresh parsley, chopped
1 tsp. grated lemon zest
Juice of a lemon

- Heat a nonstick frying pan over high heat until very hot.
- Lightly spray the pan with cooking spray, and add the button mushrooms to the pan. The mushrooms will shrivel against the heat of the pan.
- When the mushrooms are all shrivelled, add the fresh parsley and lemon zest, and cook for another 3 to 5 minutes.
- Remove from the heat, and drizzle over with the lemon juice.

Per serving: Calories: 77 Protein: 9g Carbs: 12g Fiber: 4g Sugar: 6g Fat: 1g

DRINKS

Chocolate Drink

SERVES: 2 / PREP TIME: 5 MINUTES / COOK TIME: 5 MINUTES

A versatile recipe that can be enjoyed hot, cold from chilled almond milk, or blended with ice cubes to make a smoothie.

8 oz. unsweetened almond milk
1/2 tsp. ground cinnamon
1 scoop chocolate protein powder

- Place the almond milk with the ground cinnamon in a pot, and bring to a slight boil.
- Remove from the heat and stir in the chocolate protein powder.

Hint: If desired, add 1/4 teaspoon of chia seeds just before drinking.

Per serving: Calories: 93   Protein: 9g Carbs: 5g Fiber: 2g Sugar: 1g Fat: 4g

Homemade Soy Milk

SERVES: 5 / PREP TIME: OVERNIGHT/ COOK TIME: 30 MINUTES

A nutritious drink that keeps you feeling full. Homemade soy milk has a finer taste than store-bought varieties, and is very easy to make. If you are serious about having a constant supply of soy milk at home, consider getting a soya-milk maker. It is a small appliance the size of a blender that makes soy milk from soaked soy beans and water in 20 minutes – all it needs is sieving.

1 cup soy beans, soaked overnight
5 cups water

- Combine the soy beans with water in a blender in batches, and blend until smooth.
- Transfer the blended soy milk into a deep pot and bring to a boil.
- Reduce the heat to low, and continue to simmer for 20 to 30 minutes until the soy milk reduces to your desired consistency. Stir frequently to prevent the beans from sticking to the bottom of the pan.
- Run the milk through a sieve, if desired. The soy milk is now ready to drink.

Hint: Soy milk can be drank on its own, or used to make yogurt or beancurd. The residue from the soy milk is called okara and is very good for plant compost.

Per 1 cup serving: Calories: 89 Protein: 7g Carbs: 4g Fiber: 2g Sugar: 0g Fat: 4g

Guava Milkshake

SERVES: 4 / PREP TIME: 5 MINUTES / COOK TIME: NA

Hailed as a weight loss superfood, this quick and easy recipe makes guava the go-to fruit for more vitamins, more fiber, and increased metabolism.

3 small guavas
1 1/2 cups almond milk
A drop of liquid sweetener, as desired

- Place all the ingredients into a blender, and blend until smooth.

Hint: Drink chilled, or add ice cubes to the blender to make a smoothie.

Per serving: Calories: 102 Protein: 3g Carbs: 14g Fiber: 6g Sugar: 7g Fat: 3g

Blueberry and Vanilla Protein Shake

SERVES: 1 / PREP TIME: 5 MINUTES / COOK TIME: NA

A versatile recipe that uses frozen blueberries, and can be enjoyed any time of the year.

1/2 cup frozen blueberries
8 oz. unsweetened almond milk
1 scoop vanilla flavored protein powder
A drop of liquid sweetener, if desired

- Place all the ingredients into a blender, and blend until smooth.

Per serving: Calories: 125   Protein: 9g Carbs: 13g Fiber: 3g Sugar: 7g Fat: 4g

Strawberry and Vanilla Smoothie

SERVES: 1 / PREP TIME: 5 MINUTES / COOK TIME: NA

A filling, protein-packed smoothie.

1/2 cup crushed ice
8 oz. vanilla flavored unsweetened almond milk
1/4 banana
1/2 cup frozen strawberries
1/2 scoop of strawberry flavoured protein powder

A drop of liquid sweetener, if desired

- Place all the ingredients into a blender, and blend until smooth.

Hint: A chocolate flavored protein powder will also taste good in this recipe.

Per serving: Calories: 169 Protein: 17g Carbs: 18g Fiber: 2g Sugar: 8g Fat: 4g

Pineapple and Guava Juice

SERVES: 1 / PREP TIME: 5 MINUTES / COOK TIME: NA

A refreshing and tropical drink for hot, sunny days.

1/4 cup water
Juice of a lime
2 small red guavas
1 oz. canned pineapple chunks

- Place all the ingredients into a blender, and blend until smooth.

Hint: Reduce the quantity of water, and replace with ice cubes for an even more refreshing drink.

Per serving: Calories: 100 Protein: 3g Carbs: 23g Fiber: 6g Sugar: 12g Fat: 1g

Vanilla Cafe Latte Shake

SERVES: 2 / PREP TIME: 5 MINUTES / COOK TIME: NA

A great morning pick-me-up!

---

1 tsp. coffee granules
1 cup unsweetened soy milk
4 ice cubes
1 scoop vanilla protein powder

- Place all the ingredients into a blender, and blend until smooth.

Hint: Replace coffee granules for decaf coffee granules if opting for a caffeine-free drink.

Per serving: Calories: 80 Protein: 8.5g Carbs: 18g Fiber: 1.5g Sugar: 1g Fat: 2.55g

Black Forest Dream Smoothie

SERVES: 1 / PREP TIME: 5 MINUTES / COOK TIME: NA

Crafted with the delicious ingredients of a black forest cake.

---

6 ounces water
4 ice cubes
1 scoop chocolate protein powder
1/2 cup cherries, pitted

- Place the water, ice cubes, chocolate protein powder, and pitted cherries in a blender, and blend until smooth.

Hint: Add a dash of good quality, unsweetened cocoa powder for a great finishing touch.

Per serving: Calories: 118 Protein: 9g Carbs: 16g Fiber: 2g Sugar: 11g Fat: 2g

Strawberry, Cucumber and Kale Vanilla Milkshake

SERVES: 1 / PREP TIME: 5 MINUTES / COOK TIME: NA

A great detox recipe.

---

6 oz. unsweetened vanilla flavored almond milk
1 extra small banana
1/4 cup cucumbers
1/4 frozen strawberries
1/2 cup kale leaves
4-5 ice cubes, as required

- Place all the ingredients into a blender, and blend until smooth.

Hint: Add ice cubes or cold water to thin the shake to your desired consistency.

Per serving: Calories: 137 Protein: 5g Carbs: 27g Fiber: 6g Sugar: 12g Fat: 3g

Chocolate and Banana Smoothie

SERVES: 1 / PREP TIME: 5 MINUTES / COOK TIME: NA

A weight-loss take on a much loved smoothie.

---

8 oz. unsweetened cashew milk
4 ice cubes
1 scoop chocolate protein powder
1 small banana

- Place all the ingredients into a blender, and blend until smooth.

Per serving: Calories: 157 Protein: 9g Carbs: 22g Fiber: 3g Sugar: 10g Fat: 4g

DESSERTS

Apple Cake

SERVES: 2 / PREP TIME: 10 MINUTES / COOK TIME: 25 MINUTES

A mini apple cake loaf that is sure to comfort any time of the day.

---

2 tbsp. wholemeal plain flour
1/4 tbsp. Splenda® granulated sweetener
1/2 tsp. ground cinnamon
1 1/2 tsp. baking powder
1 egg
1 tbsp. vanilla skim milk/skim milk + 1 tsp. vanilla extract
1/2 tbsp. low fat butter, melted
1/2 tbsp. applesauce
1 cup cooking apples, peeled, cored, and cut into thin slices

---

- Preheat the oven to 400°F, and lightly spray a mini-loaf tin with low fat cooking spray.
- To make the batter:
- Mix the wholemeal flour with the Splenda®, ground cinnamon, and baking powder.
- Make a well in the centre and add the egg, vanilla skim milk, and vanilla extract.
- Stir in.
- Stir in the melted low fat butter and applesauce.
- Fold in the apple slices.
- Pour the batter into the tin and bake for 20 to 25 minutes, or until the cake has risen, and is firm and golden.
- When the cake is done, allow it to cool slightly in the pan.

Hint: If doubling up this recipe, use a variety of cooking apples for greater flavor.

Per serving: Calories: 139 Protein: 5g Carbs: 16g Fiber: 3g Sugar: 7g Fat: 5g

Pecan Cookies

SERVES: 10 / PREP TIME: 5 MINUTES / COOK TIME: 20 MINUTES

This recipe uses low-calorie kamut, the acclaimed wheat of the Pharaohs, which lends its buttery taste to the cookies.

```
1/2 cup pecan butter
1 1/2 cup  kamut flour
6 tbsp. no calorie sweetener (e.g. Splen-
da Brown Sugar Blend)
1/4 cup low fat almond milk
1 tsp. vanilla extract
1/2 tsp. salt
```

- Preheat the oven to 350°F, and line a cookie sheet with parchment paper.
- Combine the pecan butter, kamut flour, sweetener, almond milk, vanilla extract, and salt in a mixing bowl.
- Divide the dough into 10 cookies.
- Bake the cookies for 20 minutes.
- Transfer to a cookie rack to cool completely before serving.

Hint: Adjust the consistency of the dough by adding 2 tbsp. almond milk if it is too dry, or 2 tbsp. kamut flour if it is too wet.

Per serving: Calories: 90 Protein: 3g Carbs: 15g Fiber: 2g Sugar: 1g Fat: 2g

Vegan Strawberry Crumbles

SERVES: 2 / PREP TIME: 5 MINUTES / COOK TIME: 30 MINUTES

A lovely vegan dessert baked in ramekins.

For the filling:
16 oz. fresh strawberries
1/4 tsp. lemon juice
1/3 cup no-calorie sweetener
1 tbsp. cornstarch

For the crumble topping:
1/2 cup quick oats
1/4 tsp. pumpkin pie spice
1 tbsp. low fat margarine
1/8 tsp. salt

- Preheat the oven to 350°F.
- To make the filling:
- Mix the strawberries with the lemon juice in a bowl, and add the sweetener and cornstarch. Mix well to combine.
- To make the crumble topping:
- Pulse together the quick oats, pumpkin pie spice, margarine, and salt until it resembles a coarse meal texture.
- To assemble:
- Divide the filling between the ramekins and top with the crumble topping.
- Bake for 35 minutes.
- Turn off the oven and allow the ramekins to cool in the oven.

Hint: Use any berry, or a combination for this recipe. It is normal for the cornstarch to appear clumpy when it in the mixing bowl, but it will set to thicken the filling when in the oven.

Per serving: Calories: 167 Protein: 4g Carbs: 35g Fiber: 5g Sugar: 11g Fat: 3g

Pumpkin Cheesecake

SERVES: 6 / PREP TIME: 10 MINUTES / COOK TIME: 1 HOUR

Deliciously soft cheesecake, suitable all year round.

---

8 oz. low fat soft cheese
1 scoop vanilla protein powder
1 tsp. vanilla extract
1/2 tsp. baking soda
1 1/2 tsp. pumpkin pie spice
1/4 cup no-calorie sweetener, as desired
1/2 cup non-fat vanilla Greek yogurt

15 oz. canned unsalted pumpkin purée

- Preheat your oven to 350°F.
- Beat the cream cheese until it becomes smooth and stir in the protein powder, vanilla extract, baking soda, pumpkin pie spice, and sweetener.
- Add the yogurt and pumpkin purée, and mix well to combine.
- Pour the batter into a glass pie plate, and bake for an hour.

Per serving: Calories: 134 Protein: 9g Carbs: 13g Fiber: 2g Sugar: 9g Fat: 5g

Easy Crêpes

SERVES: 2 / PREP TIME: 5 MINUTES / COOK TIME: 15 MINUTES

An easy recipe that can be made the night before, and used in the morning for breakfast.

1/4 cup skim milk
1/3 cup water
2 tbsp. margarine, melted
1 tbsp. vanilla extract
1/2 cup all-purpose flour
A drop of liquid sweetener/Stevia
Coconut oil spray

- Whisk all the ingredients together, and chill for 2 hours (if you can) before cooking.
- Lightly spray a nonstick frying pan with cooking spray and place over medium heat.
- Add 1-2 tbsp. batter at a time, and swirl to make a crêpe.
- Flip when the edges begin to get crispy.

Hint: To store crêpes, layer cooled crêpes between layers of parchment paper, and place inside a freezer bag. They can be refrigerated for up to 5 days, and frozen for up to 2 months.

Per serving: Calories: 167 Protein: 5g Carbs: 24g Fiber: 1g Sugar: 2g Fat: 5g

Healthy Chocolate Mousse

SERVES: 4 / PREP TIME: 5 MINUTES / COOK TIME: NA

This recipe replaces regular cream with coconut cream, and is ideal for gatherings. Although it is a healthy version, it does not compromise on the taste. To make your own coconut cream, chill two cans of coconut milk overnight in the fridge. The cream will rise to the top of the can and can be easily scooped out.

2 cups unsweetened coconut cream
4 tbsp. unsweetened cocoa powder
2 tsp. vanilla essence
Stevia, as desired

- Combine all the ingredients in a food processor fitted with a metal blade.
- Cover, and process until smooth and creamy.
- Divide the mousse into dessert cups and chill until ready to serve.

Hint: Use a spatula to easily scrap out the mousse from the food processor.

Per serving: Calories: 35 Protein: 1g Carbs: 3.5g Fiber: 2.5g Sugar: 0g Fat: 3g

Strawberry Frozen Yogurt

SERVES: 2 / PREP TIME: 6 HOURS / COOK TIME: NA

A delicious yogurt that can be served as a dessert.

---

1 cup fresh strawberries, stems removed and halved
1 small banana
1/2 cup plain low fat yogurt
Stevia, as desired

- Combine the strawberries and banana in a food processor fitted with a metal blade. Cover and process until smooth, then transfer to a medium bowl.
- Mix in the yogurt (and artificial sweeter if desired) until well combined.
- Pour the yogurt mixture into a freezer-safe container and freeze for 4 hours.
- Remove from the freezer, and stir well.
- Return the yogurt to the freezer, and freeze for another 2 hours until the yogurt is frozen.

Per serving: Calories: 112 Protein: 7g Carbs: 16g Fiber: 3g Sugar: 12g Fat: 1g

Lemon and Lime Sorbet

SERVES: 2 / PREP TIME: 4 HOURS / COOK TIME: NA

It takes a few hours of churning at 45-minute intervals to make this sorbet but it would be well worth it. Using this base technique, make any kind of sorbet with juicy fruits.

2 tbsp. lime juice
2 tbsp. lemon juice
1 tsp. lime zest, grated
1 tsp. lemon zest, grated
1 1/2 cups water
Stevia, as desired

- Combine the juices, zests, water, and desired amount of liquid sweetener.
- Transfer to a freezer-safe container until it is chilled.
- Lay the sorbet with a plastic film, and cover with a lid.
- Freeze for 45 minutes.
- Churn the sorbet with a fork, and return to the freezer.
- Repeat this process for 3 to 4 hours until the sorbet is made.

Hint: When churning the sorbet with a fork, churn also those parts that are beginning to freeze.

Per serving: Calories: 12   Protein: 0g Carbs: 4g Fiber: 0g Sugar: 1g Fat: 0g

Low Fat Pana Cotta

SERVES: 4 / PREP TIME: 10 MINUTES / COOK TIME: 3 HOURS CHILLING

A low fat take on the regular pana cotta that does not compromise on the great taste.

1/2 tbsp. gelatin
1 tbsp. water
1 cup skim milk
2 tbsp. pure maple syrup
1 cup low fat buttermilk
1 cup low fat Greek yogurt

- In a small bowl, mix the gelatin with the water and let stand until softened, about 5 minutes.
- In a small saucepan, bring the milk to a simmer with the maple syrup.
- Remove from the heat and stir in the softened gelatin until it is dissolved.
- Whisk the buttermilk with the yogurt in a medium bowl.
- Drizzle in the warm milk and whisk continuously until the pana cotta mixture is smooth.
- Pour the pana cotta mixture into six 4-ounce ramekins, and refrigerate until set, about 3 hours.

Per serving: Calories: 111 Protein: 8g Carbs: 19g Fiber: 0g Sugar: 19g Fat: 1g

Blueberry Yogurt Cups

SERVES: 2 / PREP TIME: 5 MINUTES / COOK TIME: NA

A simple and refreshing dessert.

---

1 cup low fat yogurt
1 tsp. vanilla extract
1/4 cup fresh blueberries
1 tsp. chia seeds

- Stir the vanilla extract into the yogurt.
- Divide the yogurt into 2 chilled cups.
- Top with the fresh blueberries and chia seeds, to serve

Hint: To make a blueberry compote, boil a cup of frozen blueberries with a tablespoon each of lemon juice and water, and some liquid sweetener. Simmer for 10 minutes, and add another cup frozen blueberries. Simmer again until the blueberries reach your desired consistency.

Per serving: Calories: 92 Protein: 12g Carbs: 8g Fiber: 1g Sugar: 7g Fat: 1g

Poached Pears with Rosemary Red Wine Reduction

SERVES: 2 / PREP TIME: 5 MINUTES / COOK TIME: 40 MINUTES

A touch of rosemary heightens the aroma of this dessert.

2 pears halved, cored and seeded
1 1/4 cup red wine
2 cups water
1 tbsp. fresh rosemary

- Place the pears, red wine, water, and rosemary in a nonstick pot, and bring to a boil.
- Lower the heat and simmer for 30 to 40 minutes, or until the pears are softened.
- Drain the pears, and if desired, reduce the liquids into a syrup to drizzle over the pears.

Hint: Place a small dish on top of the pears to gently press them to submerge in the liquids while cooking.

Per serving: Calories: 133 Protein: 1g Carbs: 33g Fiber: 6g Sugar: 17g Fat: 1g

Pumpkin Pancakes with Apple Compote

SERVES: 2 / PREP TIME: 10 MINUTES / COOK TIME: 10 MINUTES

Satisfying sweet and sour pudding.

---

1 apple, cored and chopped
1/2 tbsp. lemon juice
2 eggs, whites only
1 1/2 tsp. ground cinnamon
1/4 cup pumpkin purée
Vegetable oil spray

- To make the apple compote:
- Stew the apples with the lemon juice over low heat until the apples are softened. Fork mash them, and chill until ready to serve.
- To make the pumpkin pancakes:
- Whisk together the egg whites, ground cinnamon, and pumpkin purée in a mixing bowl. Spray a nonstick frying pan with vegetable oil spray, and pour 1/2 the batter into the pan. Cook for 4 to 5 minutes. When bubbles start to form, flip the pancake, and cook for another 1 to 2 minutes.
- Repeat for the remaining batter.

Hint: To use fresh pumpkins, remove the skin and seeds from the pumpkin, and steam until they are soft. Fork mash the pumpkins, allow to cool, and use as per recipe.

Per serving: Calories: 111 Protein: 12g Carbs: 18g Fiber: 6g Sugar: 11g Fat: 0g

the weight loss surgery

SLOW COOKER COOKBOOK

60 | quick and easy slow cooker recipes to be enjoyed after weight loss surgery

LASSELLE PRESS CO

BREAKFAST

All-Ready Oat Porridge

SERVES 3 / PREP TIME: 5 MINUTES / COOK TIME: 7-8 HOURS ON LOW

Pop the ingredients into the slow cooker before heading to bed, and wake up to a warm and nutritious breakfast.

1 cup of oats
1 cup of almond milk
1 cup of water
1 teaspoon of ground cinnamon
2 tablespoon of whey/soy protein powder (flavor of your choice)
1/2 cup of raspberries
1 tablespoon of fresh mint, finely chopped

1. Mix the oats, almond milk, water and ground cinnamon into the slow cooker.
2. Set it on LOW and leave it to cook overnight or on HIGH for 1 hour.
3. To serve, add more milk or water if desired. Stir in the protein powder and top with the fresh raspberries and chopped mint.

HINT: Try making your own almond milk. Soak a cup of almonds with water overnight. Discard the water, and blend the almonds with two cups of water. Sieve the almond milk through a muslin cloth. Chill and sweeten if desired.

Per Serving:
Calories: 203
Protein: 11g
Carbohydrates: 31g
Fat: 4g
Sugar: 12g
Sodium: 124mg
Potassium: 277mg
Phosphorus: 187mg
Calcium: 185mg
Fiber: 4g

Delightful Vegetarian Enchiladas

SERVES 2 / PREP TIME: 10 MINUTES / COOK TIME: 2-3 HIGHS ON HIGH

These soft and zingy enchiladas are tasty and filling, served with a burst of vibrant color!

Olive oil cooking spray, for greasing
2 medium corn tortillas
¼ cup of finely chopped yellow bell peppers
¼ cup of finely chopped red bell peppers
¼ cup of finely chopped scallions
½ cup of canned black beans, drained
2 large egg whites
¾ cup of almond milk

---

1. Lightly grease the base of the slow cooker pot with cooking spray.
2. Lay each tortilla flat on a clean work surface.
3. Mix the yellow bell peppers, red bell peppers, and scallions together. Reserve 3 tablespoons and spoon half the mixture into the center of each tortilla.
4. Now add half the black beans to each.
5. Roll each tortilla into a wrap - fold the outer right side to the center; fold the bottom up to half way; fold the outer left side to the center and roll to tighten.
6. Place the tortillas into the slow cooker pot.
7. Lightly whisk the egg whites with the almond milk and pour gently over the tortillas.
8. Cover with foil, and set the slow cooker on LOW. Cook for four to five hours or until the egg white is set. (If you are short of time, set the slow cooker on HIGH and it will be done in two to three hours.)
9. Remove the foil.
10. To serve, top with the reserved crunchy vegetables and season to taste.

Per Serving:
Calories: 174
Protein: 9g
Carbohydrates: 32g
Fat: 2g
Sugar: 9g
Sodium: 233mg
Potassium: 591mg
Phosphorus: 166mg
Calcium: 282mg
Fiber: 7g

Light & Fluffy Frittata

SERVES 2 / PREP TIME: 5 MINUTES / COOK TIME: 1-2 HOURS ON LOW

Leave the frittata to cook in the slow cooker and come back to a healthy, warm breakfast.

½ red bell pepper, finely diced
¼ cup of green onions, coarsely chopped
½ cup of baby spinach leaves, washed and torn
½ tablespoon of fresh basil, coarsely chopped
4 large egg whites
½ teaspoon of olive oil
freshly ground black pepper, to taste

1. Place the red peppers, green onions, baby spinach leaves, and fresh chopped basil in a large bowl and set aside.
2. Whisk the egg whites with the olive oil and season generously with black pepper.
3. Add the egg whites to the vegetables and mix gently to coat.
4. Pour into the slow cooker and set it to LOW.
5. Let the frittata cook for about an hour or two, until it is set.

Hint: Top the frittata with a low-fat cheese for extra protein.

Per Serving:
Calories: 102
Protein: 12g
Carbohydrates: 10g
Fat: 3g
Sugar: 4g
Sodium: 305mg
Potassium: 576mg
Phosphorus: 67mg
Calcium: 109mg
Fiber: 3g

Delicious Quinoa & Plum Porridge

SERVES 2 / PREP TIME: 10 MINUTES / COOK TIME: 7 HOURS ON LOW

Wake up to the smell of cinnamon-stewed plums in this slow-cooker porridge recipe.

1/4 cup of plums, pitted and sliced (canned or fresh)
1 teaspoon of ground cinnamon
1 cup of almond milk
½ cup of quinoa
½ cup of fat-free Greek yogurt

---

1. Sprinkle the plums with the ground cinnamon and leave to rest for 10 minutes.
2. Pour the almond milk into the slow cooker pot.
3. Add the quinoa to the almond milk and stir to combine.
4. Add the spiced plums with any released juices to the porridge and mix well.
5. Set the slow cooker to LOW and leave it to cook overnight.
6. Serve hot with ¼ cup of Greek yogurt swirled through each serving.

Hint: Plums are delicious when stewed with a mix of spices such as whole spice powder, star anise, cardamoms, and a little ground nutmeg. Consider whipping up a batch of stewed plums in the slow cooker, and serve alongside meat dishes, or as a dessert with ice cream.

Per Serving:
Protein: 11g
Carbohydrates: 29g
Fat: 3g
Sugar: 10g
Sodium: 86mg
Potassium: 311mg
Phosphorus: 197mg
Calcium: 250mg
Fiber: 3g

Layered Vegetable Frittata

SERVES 2 / PREP TIME: 10 MINUTES / COOK TIME: 5 HOURS ON LOW

Load up on your protein to start the day right, with this tasty vegetable frittata.

½ teaspoon of olive oil
½ cup of cauliflower florets
½ medium carrot, grated
½ cup of finely diced white onion
4 large egg whites

½ cup of almond milk
¼ cup of scallions, chopped
Freshly ground black pepper to taste

---

1. Lightly oil your slow cooker with the olive oil.
2. Layer the slow cooker pot with a third of the cauliflower florets, then a third of the grated carrot, and lastly with a third of the diced onion.
3. Repeat the previous step two more times until all the vegetables are layered.
4. Lightly whisk the egg whites with the milk and scallions. Season generously with black pepper and pour over the vegetables.
5. Set the slow cooker to LOW for 5 hours.

Hint: Cauliflower is low in potassium and high in fiber. You can pulse cauliflower in a food processor into rice, and use it for a low-carb alternative to rice and couscous.

Tip: If you only have a large slow cooker, use a small heatproof oven/casserole dish that fits inside the base of the slow cooker and prepare in exactly the same way.

Per Serving:
Calories: 144
Protein: 12g
Carbohydrates: 18g
Fat: 3g
Sugar: 10g
Sodium: 340mg
Potassium: 531mg
Phosphorus: 77mg
Calcium: 186mg
Fiber: 4g

Chicken Spinach & Red Pepper Omelet

SERVES 2 / PREP TIME: 10 MINUTES / COOK TIME: 2 HOURS ON HIGH

Experiment with different vegetables to add a little variety to your morning.

½ teaspoon of olive oil
5 large egg whites
½ cup of almond milk
4 ounces of cooked skinless chicken breast, sliced
½ a medium red bell pepper, sliced

1. Lightly grease the slow cooker pot with olive oil.
2. Whisk the egg whites with the milk and set aside.
3. Layer half the chicken slices and half the sliced bell peppers in the pot.
4. Pour half the egg mixture over to coat the vegetables.
5. Layer the remaining chicken slices and red pepper and pour over the remaining egg mixture.
6. Set the slow cooker to LOW and cook for 4 hours or 2 hours on HIGH.

Hint: Try serving with a bowl of crunchy cucumber salad dressed with a teaspoon of balsamic vinegar.

Per Serving:
Calories: 188
Protein: 27g
Carbohydrates: 8g
Fat: 5g
Sugar: 7g
Sodium: 580mg
Potassium: 464mg
Phosphorus: 156mg
Calcium: 130mg
Fiber: 1g

Cream of Wheat Goodness

SERVES 4 / PREP TIME: 10 MINUTES / COOK TIME: 7-8 HOURS ON LOW

An old-time favorite; this dish can be tweaked to suit both savory and sweet taste buds just before serving, making it suitable for the whole family!

¾ cup of cream of wheat
1¾ cups of water
2 cups of soy milk (fat free)
1 cup of fat free Greek yogurt
2 tablespoons of chia seeds, milled

---

1. Place the cream of wheat and water in the slow cooker pot.
2. Set the slow cooker to LOW and cook overnight for 7 to 8 hours.
3. Stir through ¼ cup of Greek yogurt and ½ tablespoon of milled chia seeds to serve.

Hint: For a savory cream of wheat, mix in low-fat cheese like grated cheddar and top with a high fiber vegetable like cabbage or celery.

Per Serving:
Calories: 218
Protein: 14g
Carbohydrates: 34g
Fat: 3g
Sugar: 7g
Sodium: 113mg
Potassium: 286mg
Phosphorus: 258mg
Calcium: 455mg
Fiber: 4g

Hempseed Breakfast Bowl

SERVES 2 / PREP TIME: 5 MINUTES / COOK TIME: NA

This doesn't need the slow cooker but is ready in a flash so simply wake up in the morning, blitz and go!

¼ cup of blueberries
¼ teaspoon of lemon zest
2 teaspoons of hemp seeds
1 teaspoon of chia seeds

2 tablespoons of vanilla flavored protein powder
1 cup of water
½ cup of Greek fat free yogurt

1. Add all ingredients to a food processor and blend until smooth.
2. Serve with extra milled chia seeds on top or a few fresh blueberries.

Per Serving:
Calories: 147
Protein: 17g
Carbohydrates: 16g
Fat: 2g
Sugar: 13g
Sodium: 129mg
Potassium: 275mg
Phosphorus: 177mg
Calcium: 109mg
Fiber: 1g

POULTRY & SEAFOOD

Thyme Turkey with Curly Kale

SERVES 2 / PREP TIME: 10 MINUTES / COOK TIME: 8 HOURS ON LOW

The kale in this dish complements the smoky flavor of the chili.

Olive oil cooking spray
¼ cup of white onion, finely chopped
½ clove of garlic, minced
8 ounces of lean ground turkey
½ teaspoon of smoked paprika

½ teaspoon of dried thyme
¼ cup of low fat chicken broth
½ cup of curly kale, chopped

---

1. Spray a non-stick skillet with cooking spray, and sauté the onions on a medium heat until they become translucent.
2. Add the garlic and ground turkey to the skillet, and continue to sauté until the meat is browned.
3. Remove from the heat and transfer into the slow cooker pot.
4. Mix in the paprika, thyme, and broth.
5. Set the slow cooker to LOW for 8 hours.
6. In the last 15 minutes of cooking, mix in the kale until the leaves are wilted.

Hint: Freeze the leftovers in serving portions. A great way to use serve leftovers is to wrap in fresh, crispy lettuce leaves for a quick and healthy snack.

Per Serving:
Calories: 116
Protein: 13g
Carbohydrates: 5g
Fat: 6g
Sugar: 2g
Sodium: 153mg
Potassium: 476mg
Phosphorus: 92.5mg
Calcium: 37mg
Fiber: 1g

Mild Chicken Curry

SERVES 2 / PREP TIME: 5 MINUTES / COOK TIME: 7-8 HOURS ON LOW

This mild chicken curry can be made a day in advance or the night before, and reheated before serving.

Olive oil cooking spray
¼ cup of white onion, finely chopped
6 ounces of skinless chicken breasts, diced
½ teaspoon of mild curry powder
½ teaspoon of turmeric
½ teaspoon of allspice
½ teaspoon of cumin
½ large carrot, peeled and diced
2 cups of water
1 tablespoon of fresh cilantro, chopped

1. Heat the oil in a skillet over medium heat and sauté the onions until they become translucent. Remove from the skillet and set aside.
2. Sear the chicken cubes in the skillet.
3. Return the onions to the skillet, and add in the curry powder, ground turmeric, ground cumin, and allspice powder. Stir to coat the chicken and onions well with the spices.
4. Remove from the heat and transfer into the slow cooker pot.
5. Add the carrots and water to the pot and stir to mix well.
6. Set the slow cooker to HIGH and cook for 4 to 5 hours/7-8 hours on LOW (or until the chicken is cooked through).
7. Serve with a sprinkle of fresh cilantro and salt to taste.

Hint: Serve with cauliflower rice for a low carb side!

Per Serving:
Calories: 164
Protein: 26g
Carbohydrates: 7g
Fat: 4g
Sugar: 2g
Sodium: 436mg
Potassium: 466mg
Phosphorus: 219mg
Calcium: 33mg
Fiber: 2g

Chicken & Summer Squash

SERVES 4 / PREP TIME: 20 MINUTES / COOK TIME: 8 HOURS ON LOW

Delicious for a quick snack!

Olive oil cooking spray
1 cup of onion, finely chopped
2 garlic cloves, minced
9 ounces of skinless chicken breasts, sliced
Freshly ground black pepper, to taste
1 cup of low fat chicken broth
1 cup of water

3 sprigs of fresh thyme
1 bay leaf
½ acorn squash

---

1. Heat the cooking spray in a skillet over medium heat.
2. Sauté the onions and garlic in the skillet until the onions turn translucent (approx. 5 minutes).
3. Now add the chicken and stir until browned. Season with the black pepper.
4. Remove from the heat and transfer the chicken and vegetables into the slow cooker pot.
5. Add the chicken broth, water, fresh thyme and bay leaf to the pot and stir well to combine. Ensure that there is enough liquid to cover the meat and vegetables.
6. Prepare the squash: Cut the squash vertically in half and place on top of the ingredients in the pot (skin-side up).
7. Set the slow cooker to LOW and cook overnight or for 8 hours.
8. Once ready, carefully remove squash from the slow cooker and allow to cool slightly. Use a spoon or fork to scrape out the flesh from the shells and return back to the slow cooker. Stir up and allow to heat through for 10 minutes.
9. Serve and enjoy!

Per Serving:
Calories: 282
Protein: 41g
Carbohydrates: 18g
Fat: 5g
Sugar: 5g
Sodium: 1057mg
Potassium: 944mg
Phosphorus: 367mg
Calcium: 70mg
Fiber: 3g

Turmeric Sweet Orange Chicken

SERVES 2 / PREP TIME: 5 MINUTES / COOK TIME: 8 HOURS ON LOW

A deliciously sweet and tangy recipe.

---

8 ounces of skinless, boneless chicken breast, thickly sliced
1 medium red bell pepper, seeds and pith removed, and finely chopped
1 medium yellow bell pepper, seeds and pith removed, and finely chopped
½ cup of white onion, sliced

1 cup of low fat chicken broth
1 cup of water
2 tablespoons of sweet orange marmalade
1 teaspoon of turmeric

---

1. Combine the chicken, peppers, onions, chicken broth, water, orange marmalade, and turmeric into the slow cooker pot.
2. Set the slow cooker to LOW for 8 hours.

Hint: Double up on ingredients and freeze half the leftovers for another meal for 2 in order to save on preparation time. Simply thaw and heat through completely in the microwave or on the stove top, adding a little extra water if necessary.

Per Serving:
Calories: 315
Protein: 39g
Carbohydrates: 29g
Fat: 6g
Sugar: 11g
Sodium: 591mg
Potassium: 1120mg
Phosphorus: 371mg
Calcium: 53mg
Fiber: 4g

Leek, Fennel & Dill Chicken Stew

SERVES 4 / PREP TIME: 5 MINUTES / COOK TIME: 5-6 HOURS ON LOW

Chicken and leek, infused with the aromatic combination of garlic, dill and fennel seeds.

1 garlic clove, minced
1½ teaspoons of ground fennel seeds
1 teaspoon of dried dill
4 skinless chicken thighs
2 medium leeks, thickly sliced
2 medium carrots, thickly sliced
1 cup of low fat chicken broth
1 cup of water

1. To make the seasoning, combine the minced garlic, ground fennel seeds, and dried dill in a bowl.
2. Score small slashes in the chicken thighs and rub the seasoning on evenly, ensuring you rub into the slashes; set aside.
3. Arrange the leeks and carrots into the base of the slow cooker pot.
4. Pour in the broth and water
5. Arrange the chicken thighs onto the vegetables and set the slow cooker: cook for 2½ to 3 hours on HIGH or 5 to 6 hours on LOW.

Hint: Try lightly toasting the minced garlic, fennel seeds, and dried dill in a non-stick frying pan until aromas are released first. You can then transfer into a mortar and pound until a paste forms. Add just a little oil, store in an airtight container and use for fish, meat and vegetable marinades.

Per Serving:
Calories: 131
Protein: 14g
Carbohydrates: 9g
Fat: 4g
Sugar: 3g
Sodium: 474mg
Potassium: 342mg
Phosphorus: 148mg
Calcium: 48mg
Fiber: 2g

Spanish-Style Chicken

SERVES 4 / PREP TIME: 5 MINUTES / COOK TIME: 7-8 HOURS ON LOW

Delicious for lunch or dinner.

---

4 skinless chicken thighs
1 cup of onion, roughly chopped
1 garlic clove, minced
1 tablespoon of dried or fresh oregano
1 teaspoon of black peppercorns
1 cup of low fat chicken broth
1 cup of water

½ cup of canned chopped tomatoes (no added salt or sugar)
1 medium red bell pepper, roughly chopped
1 teaspoon of paprika
1 teaspoon of cumin
1 tablespoon of balsamic vinegar

---

1. Place the chicken thighs, onions, garlic, oregano and black peppercorns in the slow cooker pot.
2. Add the broth, water and tomatoes to the pot and set the slow cooker to HIGH for 7-8 hours or LOW for 3-4 hours.
3. Add the red peppers, paprika, cumin and balsamic vinegar in the last 30 minutes of cooking time.

Hint: Experiment with different herbs and spices in this dish and try adding olives in the last 30 minutes for an extra Spanish feel!

Per Serving:
Calories: 143
Protein: 15g
Carbohydrates: 11g
Fat: 5g
Sugar: 6g
Sodium: 522mg
Potassium: 473mg
Phosphorus: 163mg
Calcium: 54mg
Fiber: 3g

Spiced Caribbean Chicken

SERVES 4 / PREP TIME: 5 MINUTES /COOK TIME: 7-8 HOURS ON LOW

Fragrant spices, juicy turkey and a tangy salsa on the side.

¾ cup of brown rice
¼ cup of canned kidney beans (or dried and soaked overnight)
3 cups of water
1 teaspoon of cumin
1 teaspoon of ground cinnamon
1 teaspoon of dried oregano
1 teaspoon of freshly ground black pepper,

1 garlic clove, minced
4 chicken thighs, skinless and boneless

---

1. Add the rice, kidney beans and water to the slow cooker pot and stir to combine.
2. To make the spice rub: combine the cumin, ground cinnamon, dried oregano, black pepper, and minced garlic.
3. Rub the chicken thighs with the spices and arrange them in the slow cooker pot, nestling under the water as much as possible.
4. Set the slow cooker to LOW and cook for 7-8 hours.
5. Serve with a sprinkling of black pepper to taste.

Hint: Make extra rub and keep in a sealed container somewhere dry to rub onto fishes, poultry and vegetables before cooking.

Per Serving:
Calories: 162
Protein: 15g
Carbohydrates: 15g
Fat: 5g
Sugar: 0g
Sodium: 262mg
Potassium: 220mg
Phosphorus: 174mg
Calcium: 29mg
Fiber: 2g

Turkey & Lemon Risotto

SERVES 4 / PREP TIME: 15 MINUTES / COOK TIME: 6-7 HOURS ON LOW

A delicate blend of flavours - this risotto is deliciously fresh.

Olive oil cooking spray
8 ounces of skinless turkey breasts, cut into strips
1 cup of brown rice
¼ cup of leek, finely sliced
¼ cup of chopped carrot
¼ cup of chopped red onion
1 cup of low fat chicken broth

½ cup of water
1 teaspoon of dried oregano
1 teaspoon of grated lemon zest
To serve:
Freshly ground black pepper, to taste
Freshly squeezed lemon juice, of ½ lemon
Fresh cilantro, chopped

---

1. Heat 1 spray of cooking oil in a skillet over medium heat.
2. Add the turkey breast slices and stir-fry for 3 to 5 minutes or until the meat is slightly browned.
3. Add the brown rice, leek, carrot, and onion and sauté for 3 to 5 minutes until soft.
4. Remove from the heat and transfer the contents into the slow cooker pot.
5. Pour in the chicken broth and water, and mix through the oregano, lemon zest, and black pepper.
6. Set the slow cooker to LOW and cook for 6-7 hours.
7. Before serving, stir in the black pepper, lemon juice and top with some freshly chopped cilantro.

Hint: Add a little crunch to the dish by serving with garlic flakes. Simply arrange fresh garlic slices in a single layer on a lightly greased oven tray and cook at 150°F until they are dry and slightly darkened in color. Cool before storing in an airtight container and sprinkle on the risotto, salads or soups.

Per Serving:
Calories: 145
Protein: 15g
Carbohydrates: 17g
Fat: 2g
Sugar: 2g
Sodium: 116mg
Potassium: 272mg
Phosphorus: 155mg
Calcium: 29mg
Fiber: 2g

Moroccan-Style Apricot Tagine

SERVES 4 / PREP TIME: 5 MINUTES / COOK TIME: 6-7 HOURS ON LOW

An authentic taste without the hard work!

---

2 medium carrots, diced
1 cup of white onion, diced
8 ounces of skinless chicken breasts, diced
½ cup of canned unsweetened apricots, drained and coarsely chopped (not dried)
1 cup of low fat chicken broth

Freshly squeezed lemon juice, of ½ lemon
1 clove of garlic, minced
1 teaspoon of ground cumin
1 teaspoon of ground ginger
1 teaspoon of ground nutmeg
Freshly ground black pepper, to taste
1 cup of green beans

---

1. Place the carrots, onions, chicken and apricots into the slow cooker pot.
2. Whisk together the chicken broth, lemon juice, minced garlic, ground cumin, ground ginger, ground nutmeg and black pepper, and add to the pot.
3. Set the slow cooker for 3½ to 4 hours on HIGH or 6½ to 7 hours on LOW.
4. 15 minutes before serving, add the fresh green beans into the slow cooker and allow to cook through.

Hint: Choose to serve this alone or with flat breads or couscous – just keep an eye on your carbohydrate intake!

Per Serving:
Calories: 169
Protein: 20g
Carbohydrates: 15g
Fat: 3g
Sugar: 6g
Sodium: 374mg
Potassium: 529mg
Phosphorus: 188mg
Calcium: 49mg
Fiber: 3g

Slow Cooker Rice Wine Chicken

SERVES 4 / PREP TIME: 15 MINUTES / COOK TIME: 6-7 HOURS ON LOW

A superior quality of Chinese rice wine like Shaoxing gives a nutty flavor to the chicken dish, while slow cooking removes most of its alcoholic content, creating a healthy and succulent meal.

- 8 ounces of skinless chicken breast, diced
- 1 teaspoon of sesame oil
- 1 teaspoon of low-sodium soy sauce
- 1 tablespoon of five-spice powder
- 1 teaspoon of white pepper
- 1 tablespoon of Chinese rice wine
- Olive oil cooking spray
- 2 garlic cloves, crushed
- 1 teaspoon of fresh ginger, thinly sliced
- 1/3 cup of low fat chicken broth
- 2 cups of snow peas

1. Marinate the chicken pieces with the sesame oil, soy sauce, five-spice powder, white pepper, and rice wine, and set aside.
2. Heat 1 spray of cooking spray in a skillet over medium heat.
3. Add the crushed garlic and ginger slices, and stir-fry lightly until the fragrance is released.
4. Add the chicken to the skillet and continue to stir-fry until the chicken is lightly browned.
5. Remove from the heat and transfer the contents to the slow cooker pot.
6. Add the broth to the pot and set the slow cooker to LOW for 6-7 hours.
7. In the last 10 minutes of cooking time, add the snow peas to the pot.

Hint: Try serving this dish with Chinese noodles. Prepare a bowl of cold water in the sink. Cook noodles in boiling water until al dente then plunge them into cold water to stop the cooking process. To serve, top the chicken and vegetables over the noodles, and sprinkle over a generous amount of freshly chopped Chinese flat-leaf parsley.

Per Serving:
Calories: 167
Protein: 22g
Carbohydrates: 9g
Fat: 4g
Sugar: 4g
Sodium: 510mg
Potassium: 487mg
Phosphorus: 199mg
Calcium: 47mg
Fiber: 3g

Barbecue Pulled Chicken

SERVES 4 / PREP TIME: 10 MINUTES / COOK TIME: 6.5 HOURS ON LOW + 30 MINUTES

Sweet, smoky, melt-in-the-mouth chicken with a hint of spice.

---

1 teaspoon of mustard
2 teaspoons of lemon juice
1 garlic clove, minced
¼ cup of honey
1 tablespoon of tomato ketchup

8 ounces of skinless chicken breast fillets

---

1. To make the marinade: mix the mustard, lemon juice, garlic, honey, and tomato ketchup together in a small bowl.
2. Coat the chicken fillets with the marinade and arrange them in the slow cooker pot, including any excess sauce.
3. Pour over 1/2 cup of water to allow the chicken to steam.
4. Set the slow cooker to LOW for 6 ½ hours.
5. When the cooking time is completed, shred the chicken with two forks, place back in the slow cooker and cook for 30 more minutes.
6. Serve the pulled chicken with your choice of brown bread roll and side salad.

Hint: Make your own ketchup: simply blend a 16-ounce can of tomato paste with a cup of water, an onion, a clove of garlic, half a cup of cider vinegar, two tablespoons of stevia powder, two teaspoons of low-sodium mustard, half a teaspoon of celery seeds, and a quarter teaspoon each of ground cinnamon, ground cloves, dried basil, dried tarragon, and black pepper. Transfer the contents to a large pot, add 3 cups of water and another 12 ounces of tomato paste. Simmer, uncovered but stirring frequently, until thickened and reduced by half. Cool completely before storing in airtight containers.

Please note: nutrition based on pulled chicken dish only.

Per Serving:
Calories: 150
Protein: 21g
Carbohydrates: 10g
Fat: 3g
Sugar: 10g

Sodium: 361mg
Potassium: 281mg
Phosphorus: 165mg
Calcium: 8mg
Fiber: 0g

Roast Chicken & Stuffing

SERVES 10 / PREP TIME: 20 MINUTES / COOK TIME: 4 HOURS ON HIGH

This method of cooking a roast is so simple and easy. Pop it in and wake up to a meal that's already prepared! Simply add the extra sides into the oven before your guests arrive!

½ cup of carrots, coarsely chopped
2 garlic cloves
1 small red onion, quartered
¼ cup of brown breadcrumbs
1 small (approx. 3 pounds) roasting chicken (giblets removed)
Freshly ground black pepper, to taste

1. To prepare the stuffing: blend the carrots, garlic, onions and breadcrumbs in a food processor.
2. Season generously with black pepper, and push the stuffing into the chicken cavity (use washed hands for this and get stuck in!)
3. Place the chicken in the slow cooker pot and set the timer for HIGH and leave for 4 hours or on LOW for 6-7 hours.
4. The chicken will be done when the meat pulls away easily from the bones.
5. Serve with your choice of sides.

Hint: Try shredding chicken and pair with crisp lettuce and bell peppers in a corn tortilla.

Tip: Freeze leftover servings of shredded chicken for quick go-to as a salad topping for lunch.

Per Serving:
Calories: 275
Protein: 18g
Carbohydrates: 7g
Fat: 5.5g
Cholesterol: 0mg
Sodium: 199mg
Potassium: 333mg
Calcium: 2mg
Fiber: 0.5g

Slow-Cooked Chicken in Red Wine Sauce

SERVES 4 / PREP TIME: 10 MINUTES / COOK TIME: 5-6 HOURS ON LOW

Succulent chicken in a rich red-wine sauce.

Olive oil cooking spray
4 chicken thighs, skinless and boneless
1 cup of red wine
2 tablespoons of tomato paste
½ cup of fat free chicken broth
1 cup of diced carrots
½ cup of sliced green onions
½ cup of chopped fresh parsley
2 bay leaves
½ teaspoon of dried thyme

---

1. Heat the cooking spray in a large skillet over medium heat and sear the chicken thighs until lightly browned.
2. Using a pair of kitchen tongs, transfer the chicken to the slow cooker pot.
3. De-glaze the skillet with half a cup of red wine and pour over the chicken.
4. Stir in the remaining wine, tomato paste, and chicken broth.
5. Add the carrots, green onions, parsley, bay leaves, and thyme to the pot, and set the slow cooker to LOW for 5-6 hours.
6. Remove bay leaf before serving.

Per Serving:
Calories: 146
Protein: 14g
Carbohydrates: 7g
Fat: 5g
Cholesterol: 67mg
Sodium: 278mg
Potassium: 447mg
Calcium: 53mg
Fiber: 2g

Chicken & Rice Broth

SERVES 4 / PREP TIME: 5 MINUTES / COOK TIME: 2 HOURS ON HIGH

This is a comforting, chicken broth-based recipe with rice and vegetables.

---

1 cup of dry brown rice
1 cup of fat free chicken broth
2 cups of water
¼ cup of diced carrots
¼ cup of diced leek
¼ cup of diced white onion
2 chicken thighs, skinless and boneless and diced

---

1. Add rice, chicken broth, water, vegetables and diced chicken to the slow cooker pot.
2. Set the slow cooker to HIGH and cook for 2 hours.

Hint: To cook rice with the slow cooker, use a double portion of water or chicken broth to a portion of rice, and set the slow cooker to HIGH. It should be done in under two hours.

Per Serving:
Calories: 108
Protein: 11g
Carbohydrates: 32g
Fat: 4g
Sugar: 3g
Sodium: 216mg
Potassium: 237mg
Calcium: 25mg
Fiber: 3g

Slow Cooker Lean Turkey Tortillas

SERVES 4 / PREP TIME: 10 MINUTES / COOK TIME: 7 HOURS ON LOW

Fruity and scrumptious.

---

12 ounces of turkey breasts, skinless and boneless
1 cup of canned diced tomatoes (no added salt or sugar)
1 teaspoon of cumin
1 teaspoon of black pepper
4 corn tortillas
½ cup of canned pineapple chunks (unsweetened)
1 cup of romaine lettuce, chopped
2 tablespoons of fresh cilantro, chopped
Lime dressing:
1/4 cup of lime juice,
1 tablespoon of olive oil,
A pinch of sea salt

---

1. Spray slow cooker with cooking spray.
2. Place turkey breasts in the cooker with tomatoes, cumin, and pepper. Stir to combine.
3. Cover and cook on low-heat setting for 7 hours.
4. Prep lime dressing by combining all the dressing ingredients.
5. After 7 hours, shred meat using 2 forks.
6. With a slotted spoon, top each tortilla with 1/4 of the turkey meat.
7. Divide the pineapple among the tortillas.
8. Combine romaine, cilantro, and lime dressing.
9. Top tortillas with the salad and wrap.

Hint: You can double up on ingredients and freeze remaining turkey for up to 1 month in an airtight container. Freeze in portions to ensure you're monitoring your serving sizes.

Per Serving:
Calories: 198
Protein: 20g
Carbohydrates: 20g
Fat: 5g
Sugar: 7g
Sodium: 342mg
Potassium: 465mg
Calcium: 71mg
Fiber: 3g

Slow Cooked Stuffed Peppers

SERVES 2 / PREP TIME: 15 MINUTES / COOK TIME: 6-8 HOURS ON LOW

These stuffed peppers are so easy to cook and can be stuffed with any high protein ingredients of your choice!

2 large bell peppers (any color)
3 ounces of lean ground chicken
¼ cup of dry quinoa
¼ cup of fat free cottage cheese (optional)
1 fresh beef tomato, diced and juices reserved
1 teaspoon of chopped chives
1 teaspoon of chopped fresh parsley
1 teaspoon of dried oregano
½ cup of low fat chicken broth

1. To prepare the bell peppers: cut the tops of the bell peppers off (reserve them), and remove the piths and seeds. Season the cavities with a little pepper.
2. To make the stuffing: mix the remaining ingredients (except chicken broth) in a large bowl until well combined.
3. Pour the chicken broth into the slow cooker pot.
4. Stuff each bell pepper with the stuffing until about three-quarters full and place them upright in the pot. Top them with the reserved bell pepper tops.
5. Set the slow cooker to LOW for 6-8 hours.

Hint: Try amaranth or lentils inside the bell peppers for another protein rich choice.

Per Serving:
Calories: 203
Protein: 14g
Carbohydrates: 26g
Fat: 5g
Sugar: 8g
Sodium: 207mg
Potassium: 731mg
Calcium: 65mg
Fiber: 5g

Slow-Cooked Meatballs with Tomato Sauce

SERVES 4 / PREP TIME: 10 MINUTES / COOK TIME: 2-3 HOURS ON LOW

Tasty low fat meatballs in a rich fresh tomato sauce.

¼ cup of white onion, finely diced
10 ounces of ground chicken
1 tablespoon of chives
1 large egg white
1 tablespoon of tomato paste
1 cup of low fat chicken broth
1 cup of beef tomatoes, finely diced

---

1. Mix the onion, chicken and chives in a food processor until combined.
2. Whisk the egg white in a shallow dish and mix into the meat mixture.
3. Use slightly wet palms to form equal sized meatballs.
4. Mix the tomato paste and chicken broth, and pour into the slow cooker pot.
5. Arrange the meatballs in the pot.
6. Set the slow cooker to LOW for 2-3 hours.
7. With 15 minutes left of cooking time, add the fresh tomatoes, and give the ingredients a good stir.

Hint: Try serving with zucchini spaghetti or cauliflower rice for a low carb alternative to rice or pasta.

Per Serving:
Calories: 117
Protein: 12g
Carbohydrates: 6g
Fat: 5g
Sugar: 3g
Sodium: 147mg
Potassium: 514mg
Calcium: 15mg
Fiber: 1g

Italian Chicken Stew

SERVES 4 / PREP TIME: 10 MINUTES / COOK TIME: 5-6 HOURS ON LOW

Basil and tomatoes pair deliciously with the slow cooked chicken thighs in this recipe.

Olive oil cooking spray
4 chicken thighs (boneless and skinless)
1 medium carrot, peeled and finely diced
½ cup of red onion
1 tablespoon of tomato paste
1 cup of fresh beef tomatoes, quartered
1 cup of low fat chicken broth
1 tablespoon of fresh basil, torn + extra to garnish
A pinch of salt and pepper

1. Heat a large saucepan over medium heat and spray with cooking spray.
2. Add the chicken thighs.
3. Brown the chicken on each side for 3-4 minutes.
4. Remove from the pan and add to the slow cooker.
5. Add the carrot and onions to the slow cooker and stir.
6. Pour over the tomato paste, tomatoes, broth, and basil and mix well to make sure everything is evenly distributed.
7. Season with a little salt and pepper, cover with a lid and cook on low for 5-6 hours.
8. Serve alone or with your choice of petite potatoes or tomato salad.

Per Serving:
Calories: 117
Protein: 12g
Carbohydrates: 6g
Fat: 5g
Sugar: 3g
Sodium: 147mg
Potassium: 514mg
Calcium: 15mg
Fiber: 1g

Slow-Cooked Chicken Thighs with Sweet Potato & Mango

SERVES 4 / PREP TIME: 10 MINUTES / COOK TIME: 7-8 HOURS ON LOW

A wonderful sweet and savory dish.

---

4 chicken thighs, skinless and boneless
¼ cup of canned mango (unsweetened)
1 sweet potato (yam), peeled and diced
½ cup low fat chicken broth
1 cup of water
1 teaspoon of dried oregano
1 teaspoon of smoked paprika

---

1. Sear the chicken thighs in a non-stick skillet until browned on each side.
2. Transfer the chicken with its juices into the slow cooker pot.
3. Add the mango and sweet potato to the pot.
4. Add the chicken broth, water, oregano and paprika and set the slow cooker to LOW for 7-8 hours.
5. Serve hot!

Per Serving:
Calories: 126
Protein: 14g
Carbohydrates: 7g
Fat: 4g
Sugar: 2g
Sodium: 253mg
Potassium: 267mg
Calcium: 21mg
Fiber: 1g

Tomato & Green Olive Cod Stew

SERVES 2 / PREP TIME: 5 MINUTES / COOK TIME: 7-8 HOURS ON HIGH

A taste of the Mediterranean!

---

2 x 4 ounce cod fillets
1 bay leaf
2 small potatoes, sliced into 1cm/half-inch thick slices
½ cup of beef tomatoes, chopped
1 cup of water
½ cup of dry white wine
1 tablespoon of fresh parsley, chopped
¼ cup of pitted green olives, whole
A pinch of sea salt

---

1. Combine all ingredients in a slow cooker and cook on LOW for 7-8 hours or HIGH for 3-4 hours until fish is flaky.
2. Flake the cod fillets with a knife and fork and stir.
3. Serve in a deep bowl and enjoy with a side of green vegetables of your choice!

Hint: You can use any sustainable white fish for this dish.

Per Serving:
Calories: 236
Protein: 22g
Carbohydrates: 18g
Fat: 4g
Sugar: 4g
Sodium: 513mg
Potassium: 688mg
Calcium: 44mg
Fiber: 3g

VEGETARIAN

Super Squash Stew

SERVES 4 / PREP TIME: 10 MINUTES / COOK TIME: 6-7 HOURS ON LOW + 30 MINUTES

Low in fat and high in fiber, this dish is packed with vegan friendly protein sources.

---

1 red pepper, diced
1 cup of water
1 teaspoon of ground allspice
1 cup of canned lentils (or dried and soaked overnight)
1 spaghetti squash, sliced in half vertically

---

1. Mix the pepper, water, ground allspice and lentils in the slow cooker pot.
2. Arrange the squash halves, skin side up, on top of the lentil mixture. You may need to cut the squash halves a little so that they fit snugly in the pot.
3. Set the slow cooker to LOW for 6-7 hours.
4. Carefully remove the spaghetti squash halves and use a knife and fork to shred the flesh before placing back into the slow cooker.
5. Stir and cover for a further 30 minutes before serving.

Per Serving:
Calories: 190
Protein: 13g
Carbohydrates: 35g
Fat: 1g
Sugar: 6g
Sodium: 17mg
Potassium: 634mg
Phosphorus: 258mg
Calcium: 49mg
Fiber: 12g

Mediterranean-Stewed Vegetables

SERVES 2 / PREP TIME: 10 MINUTES / COOK TIME: 1-2 HOURS ON LOW

A light dish, rich in flavors and nutrients.

---

2 cups of boiling water
1 cup of sliced zucchini
1 red bell pepper, seeds and piths removed, and sliced
1 cup of diced eggplant
1 cup of low fat vegetable broth
1 teaspoon of dried thyme

1 teaspoon of paprika
1 tablespoon of cider vinegar
Freshly ground black pepper, to taste
2 garlic cloves, peeled and crushed
½ cup of artichoke hearts
¼ cup of canned chickpeas, drained
2 cups of fresh organic spinach

---

1. Add all the ingredients into the slow cooker pot (except the spinach).
2. Set the slow cooker to LOW for 1-2 hours.
3. In the last 10 minutes, add the spinach to the top of the ingredients and allow to wilt.

Hint: Top with a swirl of fat free Greek yogurt for an extra boost of protein.

Per Serving:
Calories: 169
Protein: 12g
Carbohydrates: 32g
Fat: 2g
Sugar: 9g
Sodium: 577mg
Potassium: 1412mg
Phosphorus: 231mg
Calcium: 316mg
Fiber: 13g

Slow-Cooked Chunky Root Veggies

SERVES 6 / PREP TIME: 10 MINUTES / COOK TIME 3-4 HOURS ON LOW

Best served steaming hot!

---

1 ½ packets (21 ounces) of soft tofu
1 cup of boiling water
1 small rutabaga, peeled and cubed
2 large carrots, peeled and cubed
2 large turnips, peeled and cubed
1 garlic clove, minced
1 cup of low fat vegetable broth
1 tablespoon of dried rosemary
Freshly ground black pepper, to taste

To serve:
1 tablespoon of fresh parsley, chopped (optional)

---

1. Add all of the ingredients for the root vegetables to the slow cooker.
2. Set the slow cooker to LOW for 3-4 hours or on HIGH for 1-2 hours.
3. Serve hot with a sprinkling of fresh parsley.

Per Serving:
Calories: 139
Protein: 13g
Carbohydrates: 10g
Fat: 6g
Sugar: 5g
Sodium: 44mg
Potassium: 490mg
Phosphorus: 222mg
Calcium: 345mg
Fiber: 4g

Soft Red Cabbage & Cranberry Sauce

SERVES 5 / PREP TIME: 15 MINUTES / COOK TIME: 1 HOUR ON LOW

Delicious as a side dish, or served steaming hot with a dollop of Greek yogurt.

1 cup of red cabbage, shredded
1 tablespoon of canned cranberries, juices drained
1 teaspoon of balsamic vinegar
1 teaspoon of allspice
1 teaspoon of ground black pepper
2 tablespoons of unflavored soy protein powder
2 cups of water

1. Place the ingredients in the slow cooker.
2. Set the slow cooker to LOW for 1 hour.

Per Serving:
Calories: 158
Protein: 14g
Carbohydrates: 26g
Fat: 1g
Sugar: 18g
Sodium: 149mg
Potassium: 589mg
Phosphorus: 44mg
Calcium: 105mg
Fiber: 4g

White Cabbage & Lentils with Relish

SERVES 4 / PREP TIME: 5 MINUTES / COOK TIME: 1.5 HOURS ON LOW

This tender slow cooked cabbage is complemented with a cool, crisp relish.

1 medium head of white cabbage, shredded
2 cups of boiling water
Juice from 1 lemon
Freshly ground black pepper, to taste
½ cup of lentils (canned or dried and soaked the night before)
½ small cucumber, diced
1 tablespoon of dried dill
1 cup of fat free Greek yogurt/sour cream

1. Add the cabbage, water and half the lemon juice to the slow cooker pot. Season generously with freshly ground black pepper.
2. Add in enough water until it just covers the cabbage.
3. Add the lentils and stir well.
4. Set the slow cooker to LOW and cook for 1½ hours: the dish is ready when most of the water has been soaked up.
5. While the cabbage is cooking, make the cucumber and dill relish:
6. Mix the cucumbers, dill, remaining lemon juice and Greek yogurt and set aside to chill.
7. Serve the cabbage with the cucumber and dill relish spooned over the top.

Hint: To speed things up -remove the lid of the slow cooker towards the end of the cooking time so that the liquids evaporate faster.

Per Serving:
Calories: 180
Protein: 16g
Carbohydrates: 32g
Fat: 1g
Sugar: 12g
Sodium: 73mg
Potassium: 808mg
Phosphorus: 250mg
Calcium: 197mg
Fiber: 12g

Herby Root Veg & Quinoa

SERVES 4 / PREP TIME: 20 MINUTES / COOK TIME: 5-6 HOURS ON LOW

This is a delicious protein packed stew with quinoa to soak up all the tasty juices.

---

1 ½ cups of soft tofu, cubed
1 cup of beef tomatoes, roughly chopped
1 tablespoon of mixed dried herbs
2 medium carrots, diced
1 cup of canned pumpkin, diced
1 cup of water
1 cup of quinoa

2 cups of organic spinach

---

1. Drain and press the tofu 1-2 hours before cooking: simply remove from the package and place on a chopping board. Place another chopping board on the top with something heavy on top of that. The liquids will run out from the tofu. Make sure to place a towel underneath to catch the liquids!
2. Add all the ingredients to the slow cooker and cook on low for 5-6 hours.
3. The quinoa will have soaked up most of the liquid by now and you will be left with a succulent quinoa dish with tender root vegetables.
4. Stir through the spinach, allow to wilt and serve.

Hint: If you're not a fan of tofu, leave it out and replace with the equivalent protein serving of unflavored protein powder mixed through the liquids. Alternatively serve with a high protein green vegetable such as snow peas or broccoli florets.

Per Serving:
Calories: 190
Protein: 13g
Carbohydrates: 27g
Fat: 5g
Sugar: 5g
Sodium: 181mg
Potassium: 909mg
Phosphorus: 271mg
Calcium: 273mg
Fiber: 7g

Roasted Pepper, Spinach & Lime Quinoa

SERVES 4 / PREP TIME: 15 MINUTES / COOK TIME: 3-4 HOURS ON LOW + 10 MINUTES

Another quinoa dish, this time with a Mexican twist.

---

1 cup of bell peppers (approx. 4 small bell peppers or 2 cut in half)
1 cup of low fat vegetable broth
1 teaspoon of dried oregano
1 teaspoon of ground cumin
¼ teaspoon of smoked paprika
½ cup of canned black beans, drained

¾ cup of uncooked quinoa, rinsed and drained
2 cups of organic spinach
4 fresh lime wedges

---

1. Preheat the broiler to medium heat.
2. To roast the bell peppers, place whole peppers under the broiler for a few minutes until they begin to char.
3. Using a pair of kitchen tongs, rotate the peppers so that their skins are evenly blistered and charred.
4. Remove from the oven and cover loosely with a piece of aluminium foil. This will help the peppers sweat, making it easy to peel off the skins.
5. When cool enough to handle, remove the skins, piths and seeds of the peppers, and cut into slices.
6. Place the vegetable broth, dried oregano, ground cumin, smoked paprika, black beans and bell peppers to the slow cooker pot. Stir.
7. Stir in the quinoa.
8. Set the slow cooker to LOW for 3-4 hours or HIGH for 1-2 hours.
9. Now add the spinach to the slow cooker and wilt for 10 minutes.
10. Serve with a lime wedge.

Per Serving:
Calories: 192
Protein: 10g
Carbohydrates: 32g
Fat: 3g
Sugar: 3g
Sodium: 300mg
Potassium: 775mg
Phosphorus: 267mg
Calcium: 166mg
Fiber: 7g

Greek Rice & Tzatziki

SERVES 5 / PREP TIME: 10 MINUTES / COOK TIME: 2 HOURS ON HIGH

Rice is so simple to prepare in the slow cooker, and adding these delicious Greek ingredients transforms a boring dish to a continental treat!

1 cup of dry brown rice
1 cup of low fat vegetable broth
2 cups of boiling water
1 medium green bell pepper, seeds and pith removed, and finely chopped
1 cup of crumbled non-fat feta cheese
½ cup of sliced Kalamata olives
2 cups of organic spinach

For the tzatziki:
2 tablespoons of fresh lemon juice
1 cup of fat free Greek yogurt
¼ small cucumber, diced
1 tablespoon of fresh mint, chopped
1 teaspoon of white wine vinegar
A pinch of sea salt and black pepper

1. Add the rice to the slow cooker pot with the broth and water.
2. Set the slow cooker to HIGH for 2 hours or LOW for 4-5 hours.
3. With 30 minutes left of the cooking time, fluff the rice, and mix in the bell peppers, cheese, olives and spinach.
4. Prepare your tzatziki either in advance or when ready to eat: mix all the ingredients for the dip together and season to taste.
5. Serve a portion of the rice with a portion of the dip on top and enjoy.

Hint: Alternatively serve with hummus instead of Tzatziki and a side salad of your choice.

Per Serving:
Calories: 240
Protein: 13g
Carbohydrates: 36g
Fat: 5g
Sugar: 4g
Sodium: 417mg
Potassium: 544mg
Phosphorus: 250mg
Calcium: 255mg
Fiber: 5g

SOUPS, SIDES & STOCKS

Spicy Carrot & Lime Soup

SERVES 2 / PREP TIME: 15 MINUTES / COOK TIME: 7-8 HOURS ON LOW

A lovely heart-warming soup with a little added spice and zest.

---

1 teaspoon of mustard seeds, crushed
1 teaspoon of fennel seeds, crushed
1 tablespoon of ground ginger
4 medium carrots, peeled and chopped
1 cup of diced red onion
1 lime, zest and juice
2 cups of water
1 tablespoon of fresh oregano, chopped
½ cup of fat free Greek yogurt
Freshly ground black pepper, to taste

---

1. Heat a non-stick skillet over medium-high heat.
2. Add the crushed mustard seeds and fennel seeds and stir-fry for a minute.
3. Add the ground ginger and cook for another minute.
4. Add the carrots, onions, and lime juice and cook until the vegetables are softened, about 5 minutes.
5. Remove from the heat and transfer to the slow cooker pot.
6. Add the water, lime zest and juice, and fresh oregano to the pot.
7. Set the slow cooker to LOW for 7-8 hours or HIGH for 3-4 hours.
8. Serve with ¼ cup of Greek yogurt swirled through and black pepper to taste.

Per Serving:
Calories: 184
Protein: 16g
Carbohydrates: 32g
Fat: 1g
Sugar: 15g
Sodium: 156mg
Potassium: 738mg
Phosphorus: 202mg
Calcium: 261mg
Fiber: 7g

Coconut & Lemongrass Turkey Soup

SERVES 5 / PREP TIME: 15 MINUTES / COOK TIME: 4-6 HOURS ON LOW

This recipe uses coconut oil and lemongrass to bring a taste of the Far-East to your dinner table.

---

1 teaspoon of finely sliced lemongrass
1 teaspoon of ground ginger
1 garlic clove, minced
1 tablespoon of fresh cilantro, chopped
1 tablespoon of dried basil
Juice of 1 lime
1 tablespoon of coconut oil
1 cup of diced white onion
12 ounces of skinless turkey breast, diced
½ cup of low fat chicken broth
½ cup of water
1 cup of snow peas

---

1. Crush the lemongrass, ginger, garlic, cilantro, basil, and lime juice in a mortar and pestle to form a paste.
2. Heat the coconut oil in a skillet over medium-high heat and stir-fry the paste for 1 minute.
3. Add the onions and turkey to the skillet and coat evenly with the paste to brown.
4. Add the broth and water, and gently stir.
5. Remove from the heat, and transfer to the slow cooker.
6. Set the slow cooker to LOW for 4-6 hours.
7. Add the snow peas to the soup 15 minutes before the end of the cooking time.
8. Top with scallions and fresh cilantro if desired.

Per Serving:
Calories: 142
Protein: 16g
Carbohydrates: 9g
Fat: 5g
Sugar: 4g
Sodium: 259mg
Potassium: 383mg
Phosphorus: 147mg
Calcium: 49mg
Fiber: 2g

Turkey & White Cabbage Soup

SERVES 2 / PREP TIME: 10 MINUTES / COOK TIME: 7-8 HOURS ON LOW

Slow cooking brings out the sweetness of cabbage in this classic feel-good soup.

Olive oil cooking spray
½ cup of red onion, chopped
1 garlic clove, minced
6 ounces of skinless and lean turkey breast, diced
½ cup of low fat chicken broth
1 cup of water
½ tablespoon of ground allspice
½ cup of white cabbage, sliced
½ teaspoon of black pepper

---

1. Heat the oil in a skillet over medium heat.
2. Sauté the onions and garlic until fragrant.
3. Add the turkey cubes to the wok and sear until they are lightly browned.
4. Remove from the heat and transfer the ingredients to the slow cooker.
5. Add the broth, water, allspice, and sliced cabbage to the pot.
6. Set the slow cooker to LOW for 7-8 or 4-5 hours on HIGH.
7. Season with black pepper to taste.

Hint: If you're short on preparation time, place the cabbage, broth, water, onions, garlic, and black peppercorns straight into the slow cooker at LOW for the same cooking duration. An hour before done, add turkey meatballs to the soup instead of diced turkey.

Per Serving:
Calories: 135
Protein: 20g
Carbohydrates: 10g
Fat: 2g
Sugar: 4g
Sodium: 123mg
Potassium: 376mg
Phosphorus: 173mg
Calcium: 41mg
Fiber: 2g

Low Fat Vegetable Broth

SERVES 5 CUPS / PREP TIME: 5 MINUTES / COOK TIME: 4-6 HOURS ON LOW

This homemade vegetable broth is low in fat and can be used for many of the recipes in this cookbook.

- 2 cups of diced onions
- 1 cup of peeled and diced carrots
- 3 celery stalks, finely chopped
- 1 leek, finely sliced
- 1 garlic clove
- 1 bay leaf
- A handful of fresh herbs of your choice
- 1 teaspoon of whole black peppercorns
- 5 cups of water

1. Add all the ingredients to the slow cooker.
2. Set the slow cooker to LOW for 4-6 hours.
3. Strain liquid through a fine-meshed sieve or muslin cloth before use, and discard the vegetables.

Per Serving:
Calories: 73
Protein: 2g
Carbohydrates: 17g
Fat: 0g
Sugar: 7g
Sodium: 59mg
Potassium: 369mg
Phosphorus: 59mg
Calcium: 56mg
Fiber: 24g

Low Fat Chicken Broth

SERVES 10 CUPS / PREP TIME: 10 MINUTES / COOK TIME: 8-10 HOURS ON LOW

Use this homemade broth in many of the recipes in this cookbook, rather than store bought stock cubes for a low fat cooking option.

---

1 small whole chicken, giblets removed
3 carrots, peeled and chopped
2 medium onions, peeled and chopped
3 stalks of celery, chopped
4 garlic cloves, crushed
2 bay leaves
1 tablespoon of fresh herbs
1 tablespoon of black peppercorns
12 cups of water

---

1. Place all the ingredients in the slow cooker.
2. Set the slow cooker to LOW for 8-10 hours (overnight).
3. Strain liquid through a fine-meshed sieve or muslin cloth before use, and discard the vegetables.

Hint: You can use leftover vegetables for this recipe.
Freeze in two-cup portions to use with risottos, sauces, and as a soup base for chicken noodle soup.

Per Serving:
Calories: 86
Protein: 6g
Carbohydrates: 8g
Fat: 3g
Sugar: 4g
Sodium: 343mg
Potassium: 252mg
Phosphorus: 65mg
Calcium: 7mg
Fiber: 0g

Mixed Herb Marinade

SERVES 5 / PREP TIME: 5 MINUTES / COOK TIME: NA

A handy dry mix that can be quickly added to olive oil to use as a marinade.

---

1 teaspoon of black pepper
1 garlic clove, minced
2 teaspoon of mustard seeds, crushed
1 teaspoon of dried basil
1 teaspoon of dried thyme
1 teaspoon of dried oregano

---

1. Combine all ingredients in a food processor until a fine powder is formed.
2. Store in an airtight container in a dry place.
3. When ready to use, mix with 1 tablespoon of olive oil and baste meats/fish/vegetables or alternatively use as a dry rub for broiling.

Please note: nutrition based on marinade before oil is added.

Per Serving:
Calories: 7
Protein: 0g
Carbohydrates: 1g
Fat: 0g
Sugar: 0g
Sodium: 1mg
Potassium: 24mg
Phosphorus: 9mg
Calcium: 15mg
Fiber: 0g

Citrus Rice & Beans

SERVES 5 / PREP TIME: 15 MINUTES / COOK TIME: 2 HOURS ON HIGH

This fruity rice pairs well with curries and stews.

---

1 cup of brown rice
1 cup of low fat chicken/vegetable broth
1 cup of water
¼ cup of mango, diced
½ cup of canned kidney beans, drained

---

1. Add the rice, broth, water, mango, and kidney beans into the slow cooker.
2. Set the slow cooker to HIGH for 2 hours.
3. Serve with a squeeze of lime juice and season with salt and pepper to taste.

Hint: Serve on the side of a high protein dish such as a grilled chicken breast or crunchy tofu.

Per Serving:
Calories: 149
Protein: 5g
Carbohydrates: 29g
Fat: 2g
Sugar: 2g
Sodium: 114mg
Potassium: 181mg
Phosphorus: 117mg
Calcium: 19mg
Fiber: 3g

Mashed Beets

SERVES 4 / PREP TIME: 5 MINUTES / COOK TIME: 6-7 HOURS ON LOW

Vibrant and bursting with goodness, these are a lovely accompaniment to any main dish or salad.

4 whole beets, trimmed and peeled
1 tablespoon of olive oil
⅓ cup of water
1 tablespoon of honey
2 tablespoons of cider vinegar
½ teaspoon of garlic powder
Juice of 1 lemon
Freshly ground pepper, to taste
2 tablespoons of fat free Greek yogurt

1. Combine the beets with the other ingredients and arrange them in the slow cooker pot (reserve the yogurt).
2. Set the slow cooker to LOW until the beets are soft enough to mash.
3. Swirl through the Greek yogurt and mash until smooth.
4. Serve as a delicious snack or with your favorite high protein main dish.

Hint: To make into a purée, blend the cooked beets in a food processor.

Per Serving:
Calories: 79
Protein: 2g
Carbohydrates: 11g
Fat: 4g
Sugar: 9g
Sodium: 43mg
Potassium: 193mg
Phosphorus: 31mg
Calcium: 22mg
Fiber: 1g

Sweet Onion Relish

SERVES 10 / PREP TIME: 5 MINUTES / COOK TIME: 7-8 HOURS ON LOW

A perfect pantry staple! Leave it to cook overnight, and it will be ready to be canned for the pantry before breakfast is over.

2 pounds of medium white onions, peeled and thickly sliced
1 ½ tablespoons of olive oil
1 tablespoon of cider vinegar

1. Place the onions and olive oil into the slow cooker.
2. Set the slow cooker to LOW for 7-8 hours.
3. About an hour left to end of the cooking time, add the cider vinegar to the relish.

Hint: A water bath is an easy method for sealing mason jars. Spoon in the onion relish and tighten the lids. Place the jars in a deep pot and immerse the jars in water. The water level should be about an inch higher than the height of the jars. Set the heat to medium and boil the water to a simmer. Tiny air bubbles will begin to form on the lids of the jars, and the jars are ready when there are no more air bubbles. Remove the jars from the hot water using a jar lifter and cool at room temperature. You can test if the jars are vacuum sealed by tapping on their lids. Sealed jars lids will not rattle when tapped.

Per Serving:
Calories: 87
Protein: 1g
Carbohydrates: 11g
Fat: 5g
Cholesterol: 12mg
Sodium: 4mg
Potassium: 176mg
Phosphorus: 39mg
Calcium: 25mg
Fiber: 1g

Honey & Mustard Glazed Root Veg

SERVES 4 / PREP TIME: 5 MINUTES / COOK TIME: 7-8 HOURS ON LOW

Slow cooked root vegetables with a sweet and savory glaze.

4 medium carrots, peeled and diced
1 small rutabaga, peeled and diced
1 teaspoon of mustard
1 tablespoon of honey
½ cup of water
Freshly ground black pepper, to taste

1. Combine all the ingredients and place them in the slow cooker.
2. Set the slow cooker to LOW for 7-8 hours until the vegetables are tender.
3. Serve with a high protein entrée such as lean turkey breast, tempeh or even just a dollop of fat free Greek yogurt.

Per Serving:
Calories: 66
Protein: 2g
Carbohydrates: 16g
Fat: 0g
Sugar: 11g
Sodium: 57mg
Potassium: 394mg
Phosphorus: 64mg
Calcium: 57mg
Fiber: 3g

DESSERTS

Strawberry & Peach Crumble

SERVES 4 / PREP TIME: 10 MINUTES / COOK TIME: 6-7 HOURS ON LOW

A perfect dessert for every season!

---

2 cups of sliced strawberries
2 cups of sliced peaches
1 tablespoon of grated lemon zest
1 cup of gluten-free oats
1 tablespoon of chia seeds, milled
½ teaspoon of ground cinnamon

---

1. Mix the strawberries, peaches and lemon zest, and place them in the slow cooker.
2. Mix the oats with the milled chia seeds and ground cinnamon, and top over the fruits.
3. Set the slow cooker to HIGH for 2-3 hours or on LOW for 6-7 hours.
4. The crumble is ready when the fruits are bubbling and the topping turns golden brown.

Per Serving:
Calories: 138
Protein: 4g
Carbohydrates: 26g
Fat: 3g
Sugar: 8g
Sodium: 3mg
Potassium: 296mg
Phosphorus: 142mg
Calcium: 52mg
Fiber: 6g

Sugar-free Applesauce

SERVES 10 / PREP TIME: 5 MINUTES / COOK TIME: 1 HOUR ON HIGH

Try making this simple homemade applesauce as an accompaniment to meats, fish and vegetables or even porridge.

8 large apples, peeled, cored and diced
2 cups of water
¼ lemon, juice of
1 teaspoon of ground cinnamon

1. Add all the ingredients into the slow cooker.
2. Set the slow cooker to HIGH for 1 hour.
3. Stir a couple of times during the cooking time.
4. Mash the stewed apples with a fork for a chunkier applesauce, or blend them for a smooth applesauce.

Hint: Applesauce can be used to substitute oil for baking moist cake and pancakes. A quarter cup of applesauce can also be used to substitute an egg for many baking recipes.

Per Serving (1/2 Cup):
Calories: 66
Protein: 0.5g
Carbohydrates: 15g
Fat: 0g
Sugar: 11g
Sodium: 1mg
Potassium: 116mg
Phosphorus: 12mg
Calcium: 9.5mg
Fiber: 2.5g

Easy Rice Pudding

SERVES 4 / PREP TIME: 5 MINUTES / COOK TIME: 2.5 HOURS ON HIGH

A winter warmer!

---

1 cup of cooked brown rice
1 teaspoon of vanilla extract
2 cups of rice/almond milk
Raw honey, to taste
¼ cup of cranberries

---

1. Stir together the rice, vanilla extract, and rice milk into the slow cooker pot.
2. Set the slow cooker on HIGH for 2 ½ hours or LOW for 4-5 hours.
3. To serve, stir in a little honey and top with cranberries.

Per Serving (1/2 Cup):
Calories: 106
Protein: 2g
Carbohydrates: 20g
Fat: 2g
Sugar: 8g
Sodium: 80mg
Potassium: 89mg
Phosphorus: 51mg
Calcium: 236mg
Fiber: 2g

Poached Spiced Apples & Pears

SERVES 4 / PREP TIME: 5 MINUTES / COOK TIME: 7-8 HOURS ON LOW
Sweet and fragrantly spiced for a delicious dessert.

2 apples, peeled and halved
2 pears, peeled and halved
1 tablespoon of cloves
1 teaspoon of allspice
1 cinnamon stick

1. Turn the slow cooker to a low setting.
2. Peel and half the apples and pears.
3. Poke the cloves into the flesh of the fruits evenly.
4. Place into the slow cooker and cover with water.
5. Add the allspice and cinnamon stick. Mix.
6. Cover and cook for about 7-8 hours.
7. Remove the cinnamon stick before serving. The juices will have caramelized and formed a delicious sauce to serve with the fruits. Add fat-free Greek yogurt if desired.

Per Serving:
Calories: 84
Protein: 1g
Carbohydrates: 23g
Fat: 0g
Sugar: 15g
Sodium: 2mg
Potassium: 175mg
Phosphorus: 18mg
Calcium: 15mg
Fiber: 4g

DRINKS & SHAKES

Immune Booster Shake

SERVES 1 / PREP TIME: 5 MINUTES / COOK TIME: NA

Try this blend to boost your immune system and fight off the common cold!

1/4 cup of fresh spinach
1/4 lemon with rind
1/4 lime with rind

1/2 orange
1 teaspoon of honey
2 cups of water
1 teaspoon of freshly ground ginger

---

1. Blend all ingredients in a food processor.
2. Serve over ice and enjoy.

Per Serving:
Calories: 106
Protein: 2g
Carbohydrates: 20g
Fat: 2g
Sugar: 8g
Sodium: 80mg
Potassium: 89mg
Phosphorus: 51mg
Calcium: 236mg
Fiber: 2g

Leafy Protein Smoothie

SERVES 2 / PREP TIME: 5 MINUTES / COOK TIME: NA

No need to add protein powder, the ingredients in this smoothie are packed with protein.

1/4 cup of kale
1/4 cup of raspberries
1/4 cup of sliced mango

1 tablespoon of almond butter (unsweetened)
2 cups of almond milk

---

1. Blend all ingredients in a food processor.
2. Serve over ice and enjoy.

Per Serving:
Calories: 167
Protein: 3g
Carbohydrates: 23g
Fat: 7g
Sugar: 19g
Sodium: 176mg
Potassium: 281mg
Phosphorus: 75mg
Calcium: 507mg
Fiber: 3g

Chia Berry Boost

SERVES 2 / PREP TIME: 5 MINUTES / COOK TIME: NA

A great meal swap or something to keep you going between meals.

1/4 cup of spring greens
1/4 cup of blueberries
1 tablespoon of chia seeds

2 cups of water

---

1. Blend all ingredients in a food processor.
2. Serve over ice and enjoy.

Per Serving:
Calories: 46
Protein: 1g
Carbohydrates: 6g
Fat: 2g
Sugar: 2g
Sodium: 3mg
Potassium: 63mg
Phosphorus: 65mg
Calcium: 49mg
Fiber: 3g

Carrot & Ginger Smoothie

SERVES 2 / PREP TIME: 5 MINUTES / COOK TIME: NA

Ginger is great for stomachs and carrots are packed with Vitamin A - excellent for eye sight !

1/4 carrot, peeled
1 teaspoon of raw honey
1/4 cup of apple, cored and de-seeded
1 teaspoon of freshly ground ginger
2 cups of water

1. Blend all ingredients in a food processor.
2. Serve over ice and enjoy.

Per Serving:
Calories: 24
Protein: 0g
Carbohydrates: 6g
Fat: 0g
Sugar: 5g
Sodium: 6mg
Potassium: 53mg
Phosphorus: 6mg
Calcium: 5mg
Fiber: 1g

Homemade Tomato Juice

SERVES 2 / PREP TIME: 5 MINUTES / COOK TIME: NA

Nutrient packed and a great pick-me-up.

1/4 cup of spinach
1/4 cup of chopped beef tomatoes
1/4 lime with rind
1/2 teaspoon of black pepper

1/4 teaspoon of Worcestershire sauce (optional)
1/4 teaspoon of Tabasco (optional)

---

1. Blend all ingredients in a food processor.
2. Serve over ice and enjoy.

Per Serving:
Calories: 8
Protein: 0g
Carbohydrates: 2g
Fat: 0g
Sugar: 1g
Sodium: 4mg
Potassium: 86mg
Phosphorus: 9mg
Calcium: 10mg
Fiber: 1g

Marvellous Mango Shake

SERVES 2 / PREP TIME: 5 MINUTES / COOK TIME: NA

Delicious tropical juice drink

1/4 cup of spinach
1/4 cup of sliced mango
1 teaspoon of flax seeds
2 cups of water/fruit juice

---

1. Blend all ingredients in a food processor.
2. Serve over ice and enjoy.

Per Serving:
Calories: 25
Protein: 1g
Carbohydrates: 4g
Fat: 1g
Sugar: 3g
Sodium: 4mg
Potassium: 74mg
Phosphorus: 19mg
Calcium: 12mg
Fiber: 1g

Peach Iced-Tea

SERVES 2 / PREP TIME: 15 MINUTES / COOK TIME: NA

Ditch the latte for this energizing drink!

---

1 tablespoon of loose black or green tea leaves
1 cup of canned peaches, sliced
1 lemon

---

1. Boil a pot of water and add the peach slices.
2. Simmer for 10 minutes before turning off the heat.
3. Add the loose tea leaves and allow to steep for 5-7 minutes.
4. Pour liquid through a sieve or tea strainer.
5. Enjoy hot with a wedge of lemon for squeezing.

Per Serving:
Calories: 90
Protein: 1g
Carbohydrates: 24g
Fat: 0g
Sugar: 17g
Sodium: 11mg
Potassium: 188mg
Phosphorus: 19mg
Calcium: 11mg
Fiber: 2g

Super Green Shake

SERVES 2 / PREP TIME: 5 MINUTES / COOK TIME: NA

Kick start your day with a delicious green shake!

1/4 cup of Swiss chards
1/4 cup of sliced pear
1/4 cup of sliced apple, cored and de-seeded
2 cups of water
1 teaspoon of honey (if desired)

---

1. Blend all ingredients in a food processor.
2. Serve over ice and enjoy.

Per Serving:
Calories: 30
Protein: 0g
Carbohydrates: 8g
Fat: 0g
Sugar: 6g
Sodium: 10mg
Potassium: 57mg
Phosphorus: 6mg
Calcium: 5mg
Fiber: 1g

Apple & Banana Smoothie

SERVES 2 / PREP TIME: 5 MINUTES / COOK TIME: NA

Zesty and refreshing!

1/4 cup of spinach/kale
1 ripe banana
1/4 cup of sliced apple, cored and de-seeded
2 cups of water

---

1. Blend all ingredients in a food processor.
2. Serve over ice and enjoy.

Per Serving:
Calories: 61
Protein: 1g
Carbohydrates: 16g
Fat: 0g
Sugar: 9g
Sodium: 4mg
Potassium: 247mg
Phosphorus: 16mg
Calcium: 7mg
Fiber: 2g

Banana & Nut Butter Shake

SERVES 32 / PREP TIME: 5 MINUTES / COOK TIME: NA

Yum!

1/4 cup of spinach
1 ripe banana, peeled
1 teaspoon of almond/cashew butter
2 cups of cashew/almond milk

---

1. Blend all ingredients in a food processor.
2. Serve over ice and enjoy.

Per Serving:
Calories: 91
Protein: 1g
Carbohydrates: 16g
Fat: 3g
Sugar: 13g
Sodium: 109mg
Potassium: 179mg
Phosphorus: 28mg
Calcium: 317mg
Fiber: 1g

CONVERSION TABLES

Volume

Imperial	Metric
1 tbsp	15ml
2 fl oz	55 ml
3 fl oz	75 ml
5 fl oz. (¼ pint)	150 ml
10 fl oz. (½ pint)	275 ml
1 pint	570 ml
1¼ pints	725 ml
1¾ pints	1 liter
2 pints	1.2 liters
2½ pints	1.5 liters
4 pints	2.25 liters

Oven temperatures

Gas Mark	Fahrenheit	Celsius
1/4	225	110
1/2	250	130
1	275	140
2	300	150
3	325	170
4	350	180
5	375	190
6	400	200
7	425	220
8	450	230
9	475	240

Weight

Imperial	Metric
½ oz	10 g
¾ oz	20 g
1 oz	25 g
1½ oz	40 g
2 oz	50 g
2½ oz	60 g
3 oz	75 g
4 oz	110 g
4½ oz	125 g
5 oz	150 g
6 oz	175 g
7 oz	200 g
8 oz	225 g
9 oz	250 g
10 oz	275 g
12 oz	350 g

REFERENCES

American Society for Metabolic and Bariatric Surgery. 2016. Bariatric Surgery Procedures - ASMBS. [ONLINE] Available at: https://asmbs.org/patients/bariatric-surgery-procedures. [Accessed 01 December 2016].

Bariatric Surgery Source. 2016. Gastric Sleeve Surgery - All You Need to Know - Bariatric Surgery Source. [ONLINE] Available at: http://www.bariatric-surgery-source.com/gastric-sleeve-surgery.html. [Accessed 14 July 2016].

Bon Voyage after Weight Loss Surgery | . 2016. Bon Voyage after Weight Loss Surgery | . [ONLINE] Available at: http://www.gulfcoastbariatrics.com/weight-loss-surgery-blog/bon-voyage-after-weight-loss-surgery. [Accessed 01 December 2016].

Bray, G.A. (2012) 'Diet and exercise for weight loss', JAMA, 307(24). doi: 10.1001/jama.2012.7263.

Dining Out Tips - UCLA Bariatric Surgery, Los Angeles, CA. 2016. Dining Out Tips - UCLA Bariatric Surgery, Los Angeles, CA. [ONLINE] Available at: http://surgery.ucla.edu/bariatrics-dining-out-tips. [Accessed 01 December 2016].

Francini-Pesenti, F., Brocadello, F., Vettor, R., Bernante, P. and Foletto, M. (2009) 'P-80: Very low or low calorie diet before bariatric surgery?', Surgery for Obesity and Related Diseases, 5(3), p. S51. doi: 10.1016/j.soard.2009.03.148

Gastric Bypass (Malabsorptive) Surgery Procedure | Johns Hopkins Medicine Health Library . 2016. Gastric Bypass (Malabsorptive) Surgery Procedure | Johns Hopkins Medicine Health Library . [ONLINE] Available at: http://www.hopkinsmedicine.org/healthlibrary/test_procedures/gastroenterology/gastric_bypass_malabsorptive_surgery_procedure_92,p07988/. [Accessed 14 July 2016].

Gastric bypass surgery: MedlinePlus Medical Encyclopedia. 2016. Gastric bypass surgery: MedlinePlus Medical Encyclopedia. [ONLINE] Available at: https://medlineplus.gov/ency/article/007199.htm. [Accessed 14 July 2016].

Gastric Sleeve Surgery - Qualifications & Complications | UPMC . 2016. Gastric Sleeve Surgery - Qualifications & Complications | UPMC . [ONLINE] Available at: http://www.upmc.com/Services/bariatrics/approach/surgery-options/Pages/gastric-sleeve.aspx. [Accessed 14 July 2016].

Grocery Shopping after Bariatric Surgery. 2016. Grocery Shopping after Bariatric Surgery. [ONLINE] Available at: http://www.bmiut.com/grocery-shopping-after-bariatric-surgery/. [Accessed 01 December 2016].

Harbottle, L. (2011) 'Audit of nutritional and dietary outcomes of bariatric surgery patients', Obesity Reviews, 12(3), pp. 198–204. doi: 10.1111/j.1467-789x.2010.00737.x.

Heekoung Youn, M.S. (2015) 'Clinical efficacy of a medically supervised low-calorie diet program versus a conventional carbohydrate-restricted diet', Journal of Obesity & Weight Loss Therapy, 05(03). doi: 10.4172/2165-7904.1000267.

How It Works | The LAP-BAND® System. 2016. How It Works | The LAP-BAND® System. [ONLINE] Available at: http://www.lapband.com/r_lapband_about_how. [Accessed 14 July 2016].
Bariatric Surgery Source. 2016. Lap Band Surgery - All You Need to Know - Bariatric Surgery Source. [ONLINE] Available at: http://www.bariatric-surgery-source.com/lap-band-bariatric-surgery.html. [Accessed 14 July 2016].

Keith, C., Goss, L., Blackledge, C., Stahl, R. and Grams, J. (2016) 'Insurance-mandated Pre-Operative diet and outcomes following Bariatric surgery', Surgery for Obesity and Related Diseases, 12(7), pp. S31–S32. doi: 10.1016/j.soard.2016.08.075.

Lifestyle Changes That Come With Bariatric Surgery | University of Utah Health Care. 2016. Lifestyle Changes That Come With Bariatric Surgery | University of Utah Health Care. [ONLINE] Available at: http://healthcare.utah.edu/bariatricsurgery/lifestyle-changes.php. [Accessed 01 December 2016].

Obesity Coverage. 2016. Gastric Sleeve Surgery - The Expert's Guide. [ONLINE] Available at: http://www.obesitycoverage.com/gastric-sleeve-reference-manual/. [Accessed 01 June 2016].

Obesity Coverage. 2016. The Big Gastric Sleeve Diet Guide. [ONLINE] Available at: http://www.obesitycoverage.com/the-big-gastric-sleeve-diet-guide/. [Accessed 01 December 2016].

(2014) Pre-Op liquid diet. Available at: http://www.murfreesborosurgical.com/weight-loss-surgery/pre-op-liquid-diet/ (Accessed: 28 February 2016).

Pre Bariatric Surgery Diet by Pacific Bariatric. 2016. Pre Bariatric Surgery Diet by Pacific Bariatric. [ONLINE] Available at: http://www.pacificbariatric.com/pre-bariatric-surgery-diet. [Accessed 01 December 2016].

(2014) Pre-Op liquid diet. Available at: http://www.murfreesborosurgical.com/weight-loss-surgery/pre-op-liquid-diet/ (Accessed: 27 March20176.

WebMD. 2016. Gastric Sleeve Surgery. [ONLINE] Available at: http://www.webmd.com/diet/obesity/restrictive-operations-stomach-stapling-or-gastric-banding. [Accessed 05 June 2016].

Weight loss surgery - Life after surgery - NHS Choices. 2016. Weight loss surgery - Life after surgery - NHS Choices. [ONLINE] Available at: http://www.nhs.uk/Conditions/weight-loss-surgery/Pages/Recommendations.aspx. [Accessed 01 December 2016].
2017, wlsinfo (2017) Home › WLS Info. Available at: http://www.wlsinfo.org.uk (Accessed: 27 February 2017).

Index

A

Almond Butter
  Banana & Nut Butter Shake 267
Almond Milk
  All-Ready Oat Porridge 203
  Banana & Nut Butter Shake 267
  Easy Rice Pudding 255
  Soft Oats With Strawberry Jam 67
Apple
  Apple & Banana Smoothie 266
  Carrot & Ginger Smoothie 261
  Fresh Apple & Quinoa Breakfast 54
  Poached Spiced Apples & Pears 256
  Rise & Shine Protein Smoothie 66
  Sugar-Free Applesauce 254
  Super Green Shake 265
Apricot
  Moroccan-Style Apricot Tagine 220
Arugula
  Cabbage Soup With Arugula Leaves 150
  Grilled Dorades With A Savory Arugula Salad 69
  Salt And Peppered Grilled Chicken 114
  Tomato And Arugula Egg White Scramble 99
Avocado
  Avocado & Berry Breakfast 57
  High Protein Chickpea & Garden Pea Stew 155

B

Banana
  Apple & Banana Smoothie 266
  Banana & Chia Seed Breakfast 56
  Banana & Honey Muffins 59
  Banana & Nut Butter Shake 267
  Rise & Shine Protein Smoothie 66
Beets
  Mashed Beets 249
Bell Peppers
  Chicken Spinach & Red Pepper Omelet 208
  Delightful Vegetarian Enchiladas 204
  Light & Fluffy Frittata 205
  Mediterranean-Stewed Vegetables 234
  Roasted Pepper, Spinach & Lime Quinoa 239
  Slow Cooked Stuffed Peppers 227
  Spanish-Style Chicken 217
  Turmeric Sweet Orange Chicken 215
Black Beans
  Seared Teriyaki Salmon With A Black Bean And Green Mango Salad 79
  Chicken Simmered With Black Beans 123
  Delightful Vegetarian Enchiladas 204
  Slow Cooker Chicken Chili 144
Black Tea
  Peach Iced-Tea 264
Blueberries
  Chia Berry Boost 260
  Hempseed Breakfast Bowl 210
  Shredded Chicken And Berry Salad 119
Bok Choy
  Chinese-Style Halibut With Wild Rice And Bok Choy 84
Bread
  Golden French Toast 61
  Savory Bread Pudding 48
Breadcrumbs
  Roast Chicken & Stuffing 223
Brown Rice
  Citrus Rice & Beans 248
  Easy Rice Pudding 255
  Greek Rice & Tzatziki 240
  Turkey & Lemon Risotto 219
Brown Rice
  Chicken & Rice Broth 225
  Spiced Caribbean Chicken 218
Brussel Sprouts
  Roast Turkey Breasts With Brussels Sprouts 145

C

Cabbage
  Baked Sweet Cabbage 103
  Hoisin Chicken Cabbage Wraps 117
Carrots
  Carrot & Ginger Smoothie 261
  Italian Chicken Stew 229

Layered Vegetable Frittata 207
Low Fat Chicken Broth 246
Low Fat Vegetable Broth 245
Moroccan-Style Apricot Tagine 220
Roast Chicken & Stuffing 223
Slow-Cooked Chicken In Red Wine Sauce 224
Slow-Cooked Chunky Root Veggies 235
Spicy Carrot & Lime Soup 242

Carrots
  Airfried Carrots And Zucchini Fritters 94
  Baked Sweet Cabbage 103
  Carrot & Potato Soup 136
  Carrot & Turkey Soup 148
  Honey & Mustard Glazed Root Veg 251
  Provençal Ratatouille 90
  Tuna And Veggie Fritters 80
  Weight Loss Fish Stock 134

Cauliflower
  Cheesy Chicken & Cauliflower Bake 129
  Layered Vegetable Frittata 207
  Luxurious Cauliflower Cheese 108
  One-Pan Cod And Cauliflower In A Spiced Tomato Sauce 71
  Truffle Cauliflower Bake 96

Chia Seeds
  Chia Berry Boost 260
  Cream Of Wheat Goodness 209
  Hempseed Breakfast Bowl 210

Chia Seeds
  Banana & Chia Seed Breakfast 56

Chicken
  Airfried Chicken Kebabs 118
  Airfried Chicken Satay With Cucumber Salsa 116
  Airfried Herbed Chicken Breasts With Balsamic Cherry Tomato Salad 132
  Baked Parmesan & Herb-Coated Chicken Strips 121
  Barbecue Pulled Chicken 222
  Cabbage Soup With Arugula Leaves 150
  Cheesy Chicken & Cauliflower Bake 129
  Chicken & Lotus Root Soup 130
  Chicken & Rice Broth 225
  Chicken Simmered With Black Beans 123
  Chicken Spinach & Red Pepper Omelet 208
  Chicken & Summer Squash 214
  Chicken & White Wine Casserole 221
  Fennel & Ginger Chicken With Asparagus Spears 147
  Flourless Breakfast Muffins 63
  Grilled Chicken And Caprése Sandwich 115
  Hoisin Chicken Cabbage Wraps 117
  Italian Chicken Stew 229
  Juicy Jerk Chicken 122
  Leek, Fennel & Dill Chicken Stew 216
  Low-Carb Chicken Tortillas 127
  Low Fat Chicken Broth 246
  Marinated Paprika Chicken 120
  Mild Chicken Curry 213
  Moroccan-Style Apricot Tagine 220
  One Dish Greek Baked Chicken 124
  One-Tray Chicken And Kale Bake 111
  Red Wine Chicken 125
  Roast Chicken & Stuffing 223
  Salt And Peppered Grilled Chicken 114
  Shredded Chicken And Berry Salad 119
  Slow-Cooked Chicken In Red Wine Sauce 224
  Slow-Cooked Chicken Thighs With Sweet Potato & Pineapple 230
  Slow-Cooked Meatballs With Tomato Sauce 228
  Slow Cooked Stuffed Peppers 227
  Slow Cooker Chicken Chili 144
  Slow Cooker Chicken Curry 143
  Slow Cooker Chicken & Lemon Rice Stew 146
  Slow Cooker Chicken Soup With Baby Spinach Leaves 138
  Slow Cooker Rice Wine Chicken 221
  Spanish-Style Chicken 217
  Spiced Caribbean Chicken 218
  Stuffed Chicken 128
  Sweet And Sour Chicken 230
  Sweet And Tangy Chicken With Pumpkin Puree 126
  Turmeric Sweet Orange Chicken 215

Chicken Stock
  Chicken & Rice Broth 225
  Cabbage Soup With Arugula Leaves 150

Carrot & Turkey Soup 148
Chicken & Lotus Root Soup 130
Rutabaga & Sweet Potato Soup 142
Chickpeas
Fresh Chickpea Salad 109
High Protein Chickpea & Garden Pea Stew 153
Cod
Cumin & Turmeric Fish Stew 151
Grilled Cod With Sweet Potato Mash And Cumin Yogurt 87
Low-Fat Fish Tacos With Kale Leaves 88
One-Pan Cod And Cauliflower In A Spiced Tomato Sauce 71
Potato And Cod Stew 81
Thai-Style Cod En Papillote 83
Tomato & Green Olive Cod Stew 231
Collard Greens
Collard Greens Soup Topped With Sage Mushrooms 135
Cranberries
Easy Rice Pudding 255
Soft Red Cabbage & Cranberry Sauce 236
Cream Of Wheat
Cream Of Wheat Goodness 209
Cubanelle Peppers
Stuffed Cubanelle Peppers 131
Cucumber
Herring Salad 73
Sardine Salsa 74
White Cabbage & Lentils With Relish 237

D

Dorades
Grilled Dorades With A Savory Arugula Salad 69

E

Egg
Flourless Breakfast Muffins 63
High-Protein Scrambled Eggs 104
Peppered And Herbed Egg Muffins 105
Eggplant
Baked Turkey Breast & Eggplant 228
Lime-Roasted Eggplants 97
Mediterranean-Stewed Vegetables 234
Eggs
Vegetarian Eggs Benedict 210
Egg Whites
Cheesy Egg Wraps 60
Delightful Vegetarian Enchiladas 204
Golden French Toast 61
Layered Vegetable Frittata 207
Light & Fluffy Frittata 205
Punchy Protein Pancakes 64
Tomato And Arugula Egg White Scramble 99
English Muffins
Vegetarian Eggs Benedict 210
Tomato And Herb Pizettes 106

F

Fennel
Leek, Fennel & Dill Chicken Stew 216
Fennel & Ginger Chicken With Asparagus Spears 147
Roasted Fennel With Apple Cider Glaze 95
Fresh Chickpea Salad 109
Feta Cheese
Greek Rice & Tzatziki 240
Fish Bones
Weight Loss Fish Stock 134
Flour
Punchy Protein Pancakes 64

G

Garlic
Grilled Tomatoes With Black Garlic Spread 98
Juicy Jerk Chicken 122
Mixed Herb Marinade 247
One Dish Greek Baked Chicken 124
Provençal Ratatouille 90
Tilapia, Garlic, And Tomato Bake 85
Truffle Cauliflower Bake 96
Ginger
Carrot & Ginger Smoothie 261
Fennel & Ginger Chicken With Asparagus Spears 147
Immune Booster Shake 258
Savory Tofu 102

Thai-Style Cod En Papillote 83
Green Beans
   Stuffed Chicken 128
Green Onions
   Light & Fluffy Frittata 205

H

Halibut
   Chinese-Style Halibut With Wild Rice And Bok Choy 84
Hempseed
   Hempseed Breakfast Bowl 210
Herring
   Herring Salad 73
Honey
   Banana & Honey Muffins 59
   Barbecue Pulled Chicken 222
   Honey & Mustard Glazed Root Veg 251
   Mashed Beets 249

K

Kale
   Kale Fruit Salad 101
   Leafy Protein Smoothie 259
   One-Tray Chicken And Kale Bake 111
   Thyme Turkey With Curly Kale 212
Kidney Beans
   Citrus Rice & Beans 248
   Spiced Caribbean Chicken 218
   Rustic Bean & Mushroom Hash 53

L

Leek
   Leek, Fennel & Dill Chicken Stew 216
   Seared Salmon Fillets And Sautéed Leeks 77
   Weight Loss Fish Stock 134
Lemon
   Baked Lemon And Parsley-Crusted Sea Bass 82
   Barbecue Pulled Chicken 222
   Greek Rice & Tzatziki 240
   Slow Cooker Chicken & Lemon Rice Stew 146
   Turkey & Lemon Risotto 219
Lemongrass
   Coconut & Lemongrass Turkey Soup 243
Lentils
   Super Squash Stew 233
   White Cabbage & Lentils With Relish 237
Lime
   Airfried Chicken Kebabs 118
   Lime-Roasted Eggplants 97
   Spicy Carrot & Lime Soup 242
Lotus Root
   Chicken & Lotus Root Soup 130
Low Fat Parmesan
   Baked Parmesan & Herb-Coated Chicken Strips 121
   Basil Pesto 155
   Cheesy Chicken & Cauliflower Bake 129
Low Fat Soft Cheese
   Hot & Fluffy Strawberry Pancakes 65

M

Mango
   Citrus Rice & Beans 248
   Leafy Protein Smoothie 259
   Marvellous Mango Shake 263
   Seared Teriyaki Salmon With A Black Bean And Green Mango Salad 79
   Slow-Cooked Chicken Thighs With Sweet Potato & Pineapple 230
Marmalade
   Turmeric Sweet Orange Chicken 215
Milk
   Flourless Breakfast Muffins 63
   Peppered And Herbed Egg Muffins 105
Mint
   BBQ Sole Fillets With Parsley, Mint, And Tomato Salsa 86
Monkfish
   Asian-Style Steamed Monkfish 70
Mozzarella
   Spinach & Mozzarella Bake 107
Mushrooms
   Collard Greens Soup Topped With Sage Mushrooms 135

Rustic Bean & Mushroom Hash 53
Salmon Portabello Burgers 75
Savory Bread Pudding 48
Sunshine Pie 100
Mustard
    Honey & Mustard Glazed Root Veg 251
Mustard Seeds
    Mixed Herb Marinade 247

N

Non Fat Cheddar
    Melting Tuna & Cheese Toasties 51
Non Fat Yogurt
    Grilled Cod With Sweet Potato Mash And Cumin Yogurt 87
Nut Butter
    Airfried Chicken Satay With Cucumber Salsa 116
    Hot & Fluffy Strawberry Pancakes 65
    Protein-Packed Breakfast Bars 50
    Spiced Pumpkin Breakfast Bars 55

O

Oatmeal
    Hot & Fluffy Strawberry Pancakes 65
Oats
    All-Ready Oat Porridge 203
    Banana & Honey Muffins 59
    Protein-Packed Breakfast Bars 50
    Soft Oats With Strawberry Jam 67
    Spiced Pumpkin Breakfast Bars 55
    Strawberry & Peach Crumble 253
Olives
    Tomato & Green Olive Cod Stew 231
    Fresh Chickpea Salad 109
Onion
    Baked Sweet Cabbage 103
    Curried Zucchini Soup 141
    Hearty Shakshouka 49
    High-Protein Scrambled Eggs 104
    Juicy Jerk Chicken 122
    Low Fat Chicken Broth 246
    Low Fat Vegetable Broth 245
    Mild Chicken Curry 213
    One-Tray Chicken And Kale Bake 111
    Provençal Ratatouille 90
    Red Wine Chicken 125
    Roast Chicken & Stuffing 223
    Slow Cooker Chicken Curry 143
    Spanish-Style Chicken 217
    Sweet Onion Relish 250
Orange
    Immune Booster Shake 258

P

Paprika
    Marinated Paprika Chicken 120
Parsley
    Baked Lemon And Parsley-Crusted Sea Bass 82
    BBQ Sole Fillets With Parsley, Mint, And Tomato Salsa 86
    Refreshing Zucchini And Parsley Noodles 93
Peaches
    Strawberry & Peach Crumble 253
    Zucchini Pasta With Ground Turkey And Fresh Peaches 112
    Peach Iced-Tea 264
Pears
    Poached Spiced Apples & Pears 256
    Super Green Shake 265
Peas
    High Protein Chickpea & Garden Pea Stew 153
    Super Greens Soup 152
Plums
    Delicious Quinoa & Plum Porridge 206
Polenta
    Slow Cooker Polenta And Turkey Curry 113
Potato
    Carrot & Potato Soup 136

Potato And Cod Stew 81
Tuna And Veggie Fritters 80
Pumpkin
 Herby Root Veg & Quinoa 238
 Provençal Ratatouille 90
Pumpkin Puree
 Spiced Pumpkin Breakfast Bars 55
 Sweet And Tangy Chicken With Pumpkin Puree 126
Pumpkin Seeds
 Protein-Packed Breakfast Bars 50

Q

Quinoa
 Delicious Quinoa & Plum Porridge 206
 Fresh Apple & Quinoa Breakfast 54
 Herby Root Veg & Quinoa 238
 Roasted Pepper, Spinach & Lime Quinoa 239
 Tuna Sashimi With Lime-Chili Quinoa & Pomegranate Seeds 76

R

Raspberries
 All-Ready Oat Porridge 203
 Avocado & Berry Breakfast 57
 Breakfast Berry Wrap 62
 Leafy Protein Smoothie 259
Red Bell Pepper
 Cheesy Egg Wraps 60
 Red Pepper & Tomato Soup 137
 Savory Bread Pudding 48
Red Cabbage
 Soft Red Cabbage & Cranberry Sauce 236
Red Wine
 Slow-Cooked Chicken In Red Wine Sauce 224
 Red Wine Chicken 125
Rice
 Chinese-Style Halibut With Wild Rice And Bok Choy 84
 Slow Cooker Chicken & Lemon Rice Stew 146

Rice Wine
 Slow Cooker Rice Wine Chicken 221
Ricotta Cheese
 Luxurious Cauliflower Cheese 108
Rutabaga
 Honey & Mustard Glazed Root Veg 251
 Rutabaga & Sweet Potato Soup 142
 Slow-Cooked Chunky Root Veggies 235

S

Salmon
 Salmon Portabello Burgers 75
 Seared Salmon Fillets And Sautéed Leeks 77
 Seared Teriyaki Salmon With A Black Bean And Green Mango Salad 79
Sardines
 Sardine Salsa 74
Sea Bass
 Baked Lemon And Parsley-Crusted Sea Bass 82
Snow Peas
 Slow Cooker Rice Wine Chicken 221
Snow Peas
 Easiest Thai Chicken Soup 139
 Thai-Style Cod En Papillote 83
Sole Fillets
 BBQ Sole Fillets With Parsley, Mint, And Tomato Salsa 86
Soy Milk
 Cream Of Wheat Goodness 209
Soy Sauce
 Slow Cooker Rice Wine Chicken 221
Spinach
 Chicken Spinach & Red Pepper Omelet 208
 Immune Booster Shake 258
 Light & Fluffy Frittata 205
 Marvellous Mango Shake 263
 Roasted Pepper, Spinach & Lime Quinoa 239
 Slow Cooker Chicken Soup With Baby Spinach Leaves 138
 Spinach & Mozzarella Bake 107
 Super Greens Soup 152
 Turkey Goulash With Baby Spinach Leaves 149
 Vegetarian Eggs Benedict 210

Vegetarian Spinach Tortillas 52
Squash
  Chicken & Summer Squash 214
  Sunshine Pie 100
  Super Squash Stew 233
  Veggie Chili 91
Strawberries
  Shredded Chicken And Berry Salad 119
  Soft Oats With Strawberry Jam 67
  Strawberry & Peach Crumble 253
Strawberry Jelly
  Breakfast Berry Wrap 62
Sweet Corn
  Seared Salmon Fillets And Sautéed Leeks 77
Sweet Potato
  Grilled Cod With Sweet Potato Mash And Cumin Yogurt 87
  Rutabaga & Sweet Potato Soup 142
  Spiced Sweet Potato Muffins 58
Swiss Chards
  Super Green Shake 265

T

Tangerine
  Kale Fruit Salad 101
Tilapia
  Tilapia, Garlic, And Tomato Bake 85
Tofu
  Grilled Chicken And Caprese Sandwich 115
  Herby Root Veg & Quinoa 238
  Savory Tofu 102
Tomatoes
  Airfried Herbed Chicken Breasts With Balsamic Cherry Tomato Salad 132
  BBQ Sole Fillets With Parsley, Mint, And Tomato Salsa 86
  Cherry Tomato Soup 140
  Crunchy Super Salad 92
  Grilled Chicken And Caprese Sandwich 115
  Grilled Dorades With A Savory Arugula Salad 69
  Grilled Tomatoes With Black Garlic Spread 98

Hearty Shakshouka 49
Homemade Tomato Juice 262
Italian Chicken Stew 229
One Dish Greek Baked Chicken 124
One-Pan Cod And Cauliflower In A Spiced Tomato Sauce 71
Provençal Ratatouille 90
Red Pepper & Tomato Soup 137
Slow-Cooked Meatballs With Tomato Sauce 228
Spanish-Style Chicken 217
Stuffed Chicken 128
Tilapia, Garlic, And Tomato Bake 85
Tomato And Arugula Egg White Scramble 99
Tomato And Herb Pizettes 106
Tomato & Green Olive Cod Stew 231
Veggie Chili 91
Tortillas
  Breakfast Berry Wrap 62
  Delightful Vegetarian Enchiladas 204
  Low-Carb Chicken Tortillas 127
  Low-Fat Fish Tacos With Kale Leaves 88
  Slow Cooker Lean Turkey Tortillas 226
  Vegetarian Spinach Tortillas 52
Tuna
  Melting Tuna & Cheese Toasties 51
  Tuna And Veggie Fritters 80
Tuna Steak
  Tuna Sashimi With Lime-Chili Quinoa & Pomegranate Seeds 75
Turkey
  Baked Turkey Breast & Eggplant 228
  Carrot & Turkey Soup 148
  Coconut & Lemongrass Turkey Soup 243
  Roast Turkey Breasts With Brussels Sprouts 145
  Slow Cooker Lean Turkey Tortillas 226
  Slow Cooker Polenta And Turkey Curry 113
  Stuffed Cubanelle Peppers 131
  Thyme Turkey With Curly Kale 212

Turkey Goulash With Baby Spinach Leaves 149
Turkey & Lemon Risotto 219
Turkey & White Cabbage Soup 244
Zucchini Pasta With Ground Turkey And Fresh Peaches 112

Turnips
Provençal Ratatouille 90
Slow-Cooked Chunky Root Veggies 235

V

Vegetable Stock
Red Pepper & Tomato Soup 137
Carrot & Potato Soup 136
Curried Zucchini Soup 141

W

Watercress
Super Greens Soup 152

White Cabbage
Turkey & White Cabbage Soup 244
White Cabbage & Lentils With Relish 237

Y

Yellow Bell Pepper
Crunchy Super Salad 92

Yogurt
Greek Rice & Tzatziki 240

Z

Zucchini
Airfried Carrots And Zucchini Fritters 94
Crunchy Super Salad 92
Curried Zucchini Soup 141
Mediterranean-Stewed Vegetables 234
Refreshing Zucchini And Parsley Noodles 93
Tuna And Veggie Fritters 80
Zucchini Pasta With Ground Turkey And Fresh Peaches 112

www.ingramcontent.com/pod-product-compliance
Lightning Source LLC
Chambersburg PA
CBHW081832170426
43199CB00017B/2704